Key Topic 4: Economic and social changes 1928–39

examzone

Glossary

Welcome to the course

Welcome to Modern World History! Studying this subject will help you to understand the world you live in: the events of the last century can help to explain the problems and opportunities that exist in the world today.

There are four units in the course and each is worth 25% of the whole GCSE. Those units are:

- Unit 1 Peace and War: International Relations: The era of the Cold War 1943–1991
- Unit 2 Modern World Depth Study (Germany 1918–39; Russia 1914–39; or USA 1919–41)
- Unit 3 Modern World Source Enquiry (First World War and British Society 1903–28; Second World War and British Society 1931–51; or Post-war British Society 1951–79, 1945–70)
- Unit 4 Representations of History (your controlled assessment task).

Introduction to Unit 2B

This book covers Unit 2B: Russia 1914–1939. This is the 'Depth Study' section of your course, in which you study just one country, Russia, for just over 20 years. Focusing down on one country means you will be able to understand in more detail the changes in Russia between the February Revolution in 1917 and the start of the Second World War. There were two revolutions, followed by a bitter civil war. The victorious communist government pushed forward both social change and economic change, with a mixture of success and terrible hardship. From 1929, Russia was dominated by Stalin, a brutal dictator.

The exam for this section lasts 1 hour 15 minutes, and you must answer three questions. The questions test your knowledge of what happened, through your understanding of the causes and consequences of events, and the key features of what happened.

How to use this book

There are four key topics in this book and you have to study all of them for the exam.

- Key topic 1: The Tsarist regime and its collapse 1914–17
- Key topic 2: Bolshevik takeover and consolidation 1917–24
- Key topic 3: The nature of Stalin's dictatorship 1924–39
- Key Topic 4: Economic and social changes 1928–39

These key topics are the heart of this book (pages 6–73). When you understand them, there is a further section in the book, examzone, to help you prepare for the exam.

Key terms are emboldened in the text, and can be found in the glossary.

We've broken down the six stages of revision to ensure you are prepared every step of the way.

Zone in: how to get into the perfect 'zone' for revision.

Planning zone: tips and advice on how to plan revision effectively.

Know zone: the facts you need to know, memory tips and exam-style practice for every section.

Don't panic zone: last-minute revision tips.

Exam zone: what to expect on the exam paper.

Zone out: what happens after the exams.

These features help you to understand how to improve, with guidance on answering exam-style questions, tips on how to remember important concepts and how to avoid common pitfalls.

There are three different types of ResultsPlus features throughout this book:

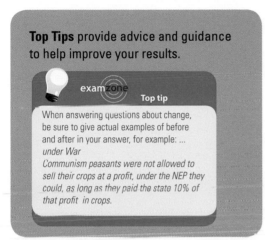

Top Tips provide advice and guidance to help improve your results.

examzone
Top tip

When answering questions about change, be sure to give actual examples of before and after in your answer, for example: ... *under War Communism peasants were not allowed to sell their crops at a profit, under the NEP they could, as long as they paid the state 10% of that profit in crops.*

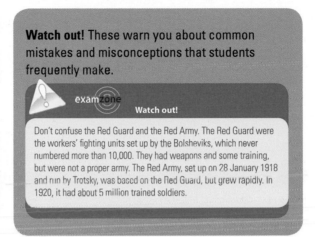

Watch out! These warn you about common mistakes and misconceptions that students frequently make.

examzone
Watch out!

Don't confuse the Red Guard and the Red Army. The Red Guard were the workers' fighting units set up by the Bolsheviks, which never numbered more than 10,000. They had weapons and some training, but were not a proper army. The Red Army, set up on 28 January 1918 and run by Trotsky, was based on the Red Guard, but grew rapidly. In 1920, it had about 5 million trained soldiers.

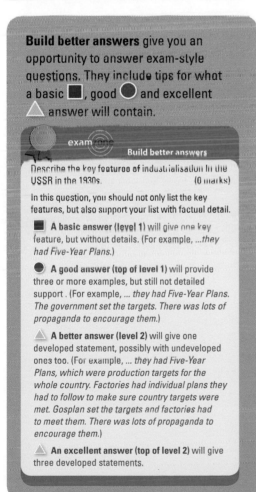

Build better answers give you an opportunity to answer exam-style questions. They include tips for what a basic ■, good ● and excellent △ answer will contain.

examzone
Build better answers

Describe the key features of industrialisation in the USSR in the 1930s. (6 marks)

In this question, you should not only list the key features, but also support your list with factual detail.

■ A basic answer (level 1) will give one key feature, but without details. (For example, ...*they had Five-Year Plans.*)

● A good answer (top of level 1) will provide three or more examples, but still not detailed support . (For example, ... *they had Five-Year Plans. The government set the targets. There was lots of propaganda to encourage them.*)

△ A better answer (level 2) will give one developed statement, possibly with undeveloped ones too. (For example, ... *they had Five-Year Plans, which were production targets for the whole country. Factories had individual plans they had to follow to make sure country targets were met. Gosplan set the targets and factories had to meet them. There was lots of propaganda to encourage them.*)

△ An excellent answer (top of level 2) will give three developed statements.

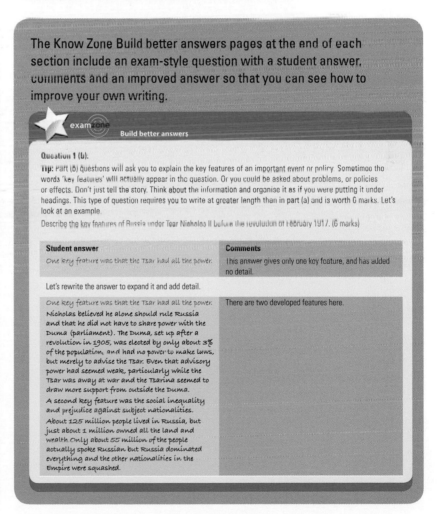

The Know Zone Build better answers pages at the end of each section include an exam-style question with a student answer, comments and an improved answer so that you can see how to improve your own writing.

examzone
Build better answers

Question 1 (b):

Tip: Part (b) questions will ask you to explain the key features of an important event or policy. Sometimes the words 'key features' will actually appear in the question. Or you could be asked about problems, or policies or effects. Don't just tell the story. Think about the information and organise it as if you were putting it under headings. This type of question requires you to write at greater length than in part (a) and is worth 6 marks. Let's look at an example.

Describe the key features of Russia under Tsar Nicholas II before the revolution of February 1917. (6 marks)

Student answer	Comments
One key feature was that the Tsar had all the power.	This answer gives only one key feature, and has added no detail.

Let's rewrite the answer to expand it and add detail.

One key feature was that the Tsar had all the power. Nicholas believed he alone should rule Russia and that he did not have to share power with the Duma (parliament). The Duma, set up after a revolution in 1905, was elected by only about 3% of the population, and had no power to make laws, but merely to advise the Tsar. Even that advisory power had seemed weak, particularly while the Tsar was away at war and the Tsarina seemed to draw more support from outside the Duma. A second key feature was the social inequality and prejudice against subject nationalities. About 125 million people lived in Russia, but just about 1 million owned all the land and wealth. Only about 55 million of the people actually spoke Russian but Russia dominated everything and the other nationalities in the Empire were squashed.	There are two developed features here.

Key Topic 1: The Tsarist regime and its collapse 1914–17

Russia in 1914 was a vast country with a huge population. It was a country of enormous social inequality; most of the wealth and all of the power belonged to about 1 million of its 125.6 million people. Tsar Nicholas II, the ruler of Russia, was unpopular because, despite a revolution in 1905, he had failed to carry out all the reforms to the way Russia was run that people wanted.

In August 1914, the First World War broke out between Russia, France and Britain (the Triple Entente) and Germany, Austria-Hungary and Italy (the Triple Alliance). After some initial success in the war, Russia suffered huge losses. The Tsar's conduct of the war made him more unpopular. There were shortages of food, fuel and other supplies. People starved. In February 1917, the country erupted into revolution. The Tsar tried to return to the capital, Petrograd, from the front. It was too late; his government was no longer in control and he had to abdicate. A new Provisional Government was formed and Russia was now a republic.

In this Key Topic you will study:

- the nature of Tsarist rule
- the impact of the First World War
- the fall of the Tsar.

Russia in 1914

> ### Learning objectives
>
> In this chapter you will learn about:
> - the problems of ruling Russia
> - the social and economic problems
> - the weakness of the Tsar.

The problems of ruling Russia

The Russian Empire in 1914 was huge, 92 times as big as Britain. It stretched from Europe in the west to the Pacific Ocean in the east and from the Arctic Ocean in the north to Afghanistan in the south. It covered about 22.3 million square km, about a sixth of all the land in the world. Its size made it very hard to govern. Communications were difficult. Roads were unpaved and slow, thick with mud for much of the year in many places. Even the new railways only connected a fraction of the country.

Communication was difficult in another way, too. In 1897, when its only census was taken, Russia had over 125.6 million people. Of these, only about 55 million spoke Russian. Despite this, Russian was the language of government and people were expected to conform to Russian ways, in a process called 'Russification'. There were hundreds of different nationalities, living in very different ways in climates that ranged from desert to permanent ice. They had one thing in common – they were almost all peasants.

Social problems

The 1897 census showed terrible **social inequality** in Russia. Over half of the peasants had no land or homes of their own. Much of the farmland was of poor quality and farmed with old-fashioned, ineffective methods. The population was rising and more people were moving to towns, so more food was needed and food shortages were common. Most of the land, most of the wealth and all of the power belonged to about 1 million of the 125.6 million people. These people did not go hungry when there were food shortages.

Source A: *a photograph taken by a visitor to a Russian village in the early 1900s.*

Occupation	Population in millions
Peasants	93.7
Factory workers	12.3
Shopkeepers	5.0
Railway and communications	1.9
Servants and workers hired by the day	5.8
Priests and professionals	1.6
Government officials, soldiers	2.2
Landlords, nobles etc	2.2
Criminals and other unknowns	0.9

Source B: *the occupation of Russians in the 1897 census.*

> ### Exam-style question
>
> **Describe the problems of ruling Russia in 1917.**
> **(6 marks)**
>
> **Tip:** Pick out at least three problems, and don't just list them, explain what made them a problem.

Town life

More and more peasants were moving to towns and cities to look for work in factories. Moscow, with a total population of 1.8 million, was the most **industrialised** city: just under 50% of all factory workers worked there. Life in the towns was not easy. Work was difficult to find. The hours were long, the pay was low and the work was hard and dangerous – accidents were common. Factory workers lived in the worst part of the town, often ten to a room, taking it in turns to sleep. Despite all this, for many it was better than being a peasant. Factory owners, on the other hand, lived well. They made huge profits by paying low wages and they spent very little on improving living or working conditions for their workers.

How Russia was ruled

Russia was ruled by a **Tsar** who made all the decisions, advised by a Council of Ministers chosen from his friends in the nobility. Since 1613, the Tsar had always come from the Romanov family. The Russian Orthodox Church supported the Tsars and encouraged the belief that they were above criticism and chosen to rule by God: people should always obey the Tsar and his officials. Nicholas II became Tsar in 1894. He was an indecisive man who, when told he had become Tsar, had said, 'I am not ready to be Tsar. I know nothing about the business of ruling.' He certainly did not think enough about the problems of Russia. Books and newspapers were censored to make sure they were not hostile. A secret police, the **Okhrana**, looked for opponents of the Tsar. These people were usually exiled to Siberia, 3,000 miles away in the icy north. Other critics left the country.

The 1905 Revolution

In 1905 there was a series of demonstrations and strikes against the way things were. Troops guarding the Tsar's Winter Palace in St Petersburg fired into a crowd of peaceful demonstrators, killing 130 and wounding many more. This produced more strikes and more unrest. The St Petersburg strikers formed a soviet – a workers' council to organise strikes. Work in the city stopped. Soviets were organised in more and more towns and cities. They took over in some places, replacing the Tsar's government.

Source C: *a soup kitchen for the unemployed in St Petersburg in the early 1900s. Soup kitchens provided a very basic meal for the unemployed, usually once a day.*

At times in 1905 the government lost control of some towns, cities and areas, as industrial workers staged huge strikes. There were repeated mutinies in the army and the navy. A nationwide general strike in October brought the country to a near standstill.

Source D: *from* The Soviet Experiment, *written by R G Suny in 1998.*

A second chance

Nicholas II had to act quickly to survive. He set up a Duma (parliament) of two Houses, one elected by the people and the other of nobles appointed by the Tsar, to advise him. He agreed to allow political parties and trade unions (these had been illegal). Many groups that had met in secret began to hold public meetings and demand reforms. These included the soviets, which still had a lot of public support in the towns and cities, especially St Petersburg. Opposition to the Tsar was now more obvious.

Rasputin

The Tsar and Tsarina's only son, Alexi, had haemophilia, a medical condition that stops blood clotting. At the time, there were no drugs to control this condition so even small cuts and bruises were a problem and could be fatal. Alexi's condition was kept secret from almost everyone.

In 1905 the Tsar and Tsarina first heard of a 'holy man' called Rasputin, who could help with haemophilia. In 1907, Alexi was very ill and Rasputin was called for. He stopped the bleeding. The Tsar and Tsarina came to rely on Rasputin more and more. He was very unpopular, even in the Tsar's court, because of his growing influence over them. No one understood it, because hardly anyone knew of Alexi's condition. Some disliked Rasputin because he was from a peasant family, others because they thought he was a fraud. But he seemed to help Alexi. So, despite protests, the Tsar and Tsarina protected him and kept him at court.

Back to the old ways

Tsar Nicolas did not want to share power as he believed that God had given him the right to rule alone. There was a huge difference between what he had promised in October 1905 and what he would really allow. When the Duma began to demand reforms he changed the voting system for the Duma, trying to make sure only people who would agree with him were elected.

As time passed, the Tsar began to feel safe again. He stopped calling the Duma at all, as even though it was elected by his new rules, it still wanted reform. By 1907 the Okhrana was openly breaking up the meetings of political parties and trade unions, even though these meetings were legal. Leaders were arrested on false charges and sent to prison, or to exile in Siberia. The persecution was intended to break up these groups, and it partly succeeded.

Many political groups returned to meeting in secret. Some had to work in exile, while others left the country. Many small soviets still met, but the St Petersburg Soviet, which had been the most influential (so was most persecuted) stopped meeting in 1905.

Source E: *a Russian cartoon from the time, showing how many Russians thought Rasputin controlled the Tsar and Tsarina.*

Opposition

Opposition to the Tsar's new government after the changes of 1905 fell into four main groups:

- **Monarchists** who wanted a return to the Tsar ruling alone. They disliked the new government that included the Duma.
- **Constitutionalists** who wanted to keep the Tsar, but limit his power with a constitution and some kind of parliament. The most important were the Constitutional Democratic Party (the Kadets), the Octobrists and the Progressists. Most members of the first Dumas (before the Tsar changed the voting system) came from these parties.
- **Revolutionaries** who wanted to replace the Tsarist system with a fairer one. The largest group was the Social Revolutionaries, who believed in a revolution led by the peasants. Some revolutionary parties followed the ideas of the revolutionary socialist, Karl Marx. The largest of these, the Social Democrats, believed in a revolution led by the workers in the towns and cities. Many of these groups were exiled when the Okhrana stepped up its persecution.
- **Soviets** who wanted reforms to help ordinary workers. They were loyal to the Tsar at first; they just wanted him to see their problems and help. This view changed as it became clear he was not interested in their problems.

Problems outside Russia

Europe at the start of 1914 was a tangle of alliances. Germany, Austria-Hungary and Italy had formed the Triple Alliance. Russia, Britain and France had formed the Triple Entente. All these countries had treaties with smaller ones. One of Russia's allies was Serbia, a country in the Balkans that wanted independence from Austria-Hungary. When the heir to Austria's throne, Franz Ferdinand, was assassinated in Sarajevo by a Serbian independence group, Austria declared war on Serbia. Russia had promised to protect Serbia, so

joined the war, bringing in France and Britain. Meanwhile Italy and Germany joined in to help Austria-Hungary. Other countries followed, hauled in by treaties.

The First World War had begun.

Soviets
What
'Soviet' is the Russian word for a Council or Committee. The lowest level soviets were set up by workers in a factory, or soldiers in a unit. All the soviets in a city could join together to form a city soviet, like the St Petersburg Soviet. Each smaller soviet sent some representatives to sit on the city soviet.
Why
To start with, soviets were not much more than strike committees. However, revolutionaries soon realised they were the best way to organise the workers, and so get some real power. **Bolsheviks** tried to make sure they were among the leaders of all soviets.
When
1905 used by St Petersburg workers in the failed revolution.
1917 an important part of the February Revolution. Eventually (September) dominated by radicals, especially the Bolsheviks, they were a threat to the Provisional Government – and more representative of the people.
After the revolution the constitution made them part of the system of government. Soviets elected members to larger soviets all the way up to the Supreme Soviet – the top level of the government.

examzone
Watch out!

The capital of Russia until 1918 was St Petersburg, but in 1914 the name of the city was changed to Petrograd. In 1924, the name was changed again to Leningrad. Remember these three names all refer to the same place but at different times.

Activities

1 Draw a diagram to show what would happen if there was a revolution in your school, and it was run by soviets. What would be the smallest soviet, and how many levels of soviets would you need?

2 **a** In pairs, write the problems in Russia onto small cards. Now sort them into two piles: *geographical problems* and *political problems*.

  b Pick the problem you think is most likely to lead to revolution and write a paragraph explaining why.

3 Write a slogan for each of the main political parties in 1917.

The First World War

At first, people supported the war. Most of the Duma voted for more taxes to pay for it with only 21 deputies voting against, and strikes almost stopped. St Petersburg (which sounded too German) was re-named Petrograd. However, the Tsarina, already disliked for her reliance on Rasputin, came under more suspicion because she was German.

The Russian army invaded East Prussia in August from the south-west and the north-east at the same time. Due to the huge size of the Russian army it had some initial success, such as at Gumbinnen where it drove the Germans back.

Early success was followed by a stunning defeat by the Germans at Tannenberg in late August. Of the 150,000 Russian soldiers that began the battle, over 30,000 were killed and over 92,000 captured. Vast amounts of weapons were captured too – it took six trains to carry the captured equipment back to Germany. Worse was to follow. Two defeats at the Masurian Lakes (September 1914 and February 1915) also resulted in huge losses. Russia's size, poor transport systems and inefficient industry all put Russia at a disadvantage, as did poor training and shortages of equipment. Some Russian soldiers had no weapons as they went into battle – they were told to pick up weapons dropped by shot comrades. By August 1915 over 2 million men were dead, wounded or prisoners. Most of four provinces, including a major coal-mining district, were captured by the Germans.

Source A: *A German army train loaded with Russian weapons and equipment after the Masurian Lakes campaign.*

Tsar Nicholas takes control

On 5 September 1915, the Tsar took personal command of the army as Commander-in-Chief. He did this against the advice of his cabinet and it made his situation worse. The war went no better – and now the Tsar, not his commanders, was blamed for it. His popularity, which had risen at the start of the war, dropped. Also, he left his wife as his deputy in Petrograd despite her unpopularity. She, in turn, made matters worse by relying on the advice of Rasputin, not the Tsar's official advisers. Not only that, she sacked several of these advisors. Rumours grew that she and Rasputin were working for the Germans and that they were lovers. The royal family was losing a lot of support. In December 1916 a group of nobles assassinated Rasputin, to end what they saw as his disastrous influence over the royal family. However, the damage was already done.

Effects of the war

The war made all the problems that Russia had had before the war worse. By 1917, over 15 million Russian men had joined the army - mostly because they were **conscripted**. Millions of horses, needed for transportation, had been taken from farms. Soldiers at the Front were given priority for food and other supplies and factories turned to war production. People were told to move to the towns to work in the factories producing war materials. These actions had wide-reaching effects.

- Millions of peasants left farming, through conscription and moving workers into war work in factories. With horses gone too, farming became more difficult, as did transporting crops. Food production dropped.
- Fertilizer factories switched to war work, so there was less fertilizer. Food production dropped further.
- Millions of trained factory workers were conscripted. Their replacements were inexperienced. Production dropped and the quality of goods suffered.
- The number of people living in towns rose by about 6 million from 1914 to 1917. These people all needed to buy food, fuel and other basic goods. With not enough housing for these extra people, slums developed.
- Inflation struck. Shortages pushed the prices of most goods up sharply. The government made things worse by printing more money to cover its own spending on the war. As there was more money in circulation and fewer goods, prices continued to rise. From 1915, riots in cities due to shortages became more and more frequent and serious. The crime rate in towns and cities in 1917 was three times what it had been in 1914.

Year	Men in the army (in millions)	Percentage of all men of working age
1914	6.5	14.9%
1915	11.2	25.2%
1916	14.2	35.7%
1917	15.1	36.7%

Source B: *Russia's army, 1914–17.*

Of the 15 million who by early 1917 had been in the army, 1.8m were dead, 3.9m wounded, and 2.4m prisoners. Ill-equipped, ill-treated, and ill-used, the Russian soldier had had enough.

Source C: *from a 1998 history of the First World War.*

The railways were timetabled to run from east to west to supply the army. Food for the major industrial centres travelled from south to north. As the army always came first, food often ended up rotting in goods wagons waiting for an engine to take them to Moscow or Petrograd.

Source D: *from A People's Tragedy, a 1996 history of the Russian revolution by Orlando Figes.*

Exam-style question

Explain the effects of the First World War on Russia up to 1917. **(8 marks)**
Tip: When asked to explain effects don't just list them, explain a little about each one. Activity 1 to the right is a good way to practise this.

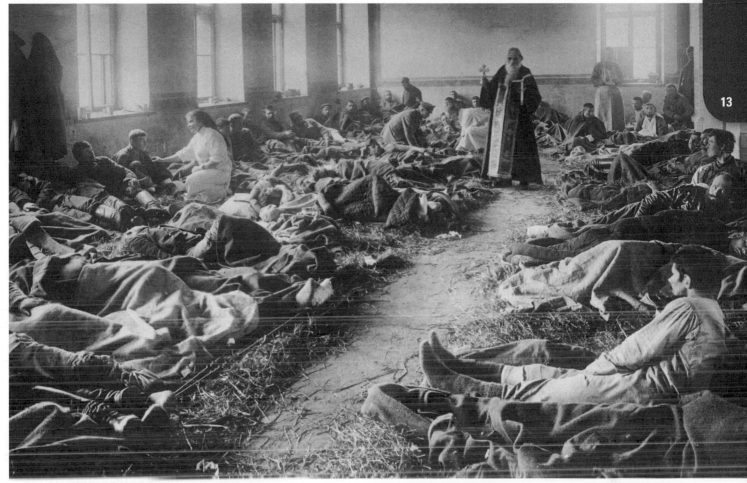

Source E: *wounded soldiers in a Russian military hospital*

Ready to revolt

Political opponents of the Tsar began to be openly critical of his rule once more. The Okhrana no longer had the control over people it had had in 1914. The actions of the Tsar and Tsarina had made them unpopular and, under the Tsarina, the government was disunited and unpopular too.

The leaders of the soviets in the towns and cities, often Bolsheviks or **Mensheviks**, were quick to respond to the worsening conditions and the growing lack of government control. They held public meetings about the shortages, the deaths at the front, government incompetence. They talked about revolution and more and more people listened. People no longer gave the Tsar the automatic loyalty they once had. They no longer believed that he loved his people. They stopped using excuses for him, such as that he was 'badly advised'. This loyalty had been one of the factors that had stopped people short of open revolt before. Now it was gone.

Activities

1 In history answers, you often need to make general points, then to support them with more detail. To practise this skill, in this exercise you are given four general statements. Copy each one, then pick out and list some detail to support it. For example:

   At the start, the war was popular.

   - *Only 21 deputies did not vote for the taxes.*
   - *There were almost no strikes for the first year of the war.*

   a The Tsar and his government were not good at running the war.

   b The war made Russia's food problems worse.

   c The war made Russia's industry less effective.

   d The war made people more likely to join a revolt against the Tsar and his government.

2 In pairs, discuss which of Sources A–E is the best illustration of Russia's problems. Does everybody else in your group agree?

Revolution!

> ### Learning objectives
>
> In this chapter you will learn about:
> - the events of the February Revolution
> - why the Tsar was overthrown.

The first few months of 1917 were colder than usual. The temperature in Petrograd fell to an average of −15˚C. It was too cold for trains to run. People often queued all night for bread, only to find the baker had not baked because he had either no fuel or no flour. Strikes and demonstrations broke out in several cities. On 19 February, government officials in Petrograd announced rationing would start on 1 March. On 21 February, managers of the Putilov Works (the biggest factory in Petrograd) **locked-out** some workers. This set off a strike. The strike spread to other factories in the area.

Growing unrest

On 23 February Russia celebrated International Women's Day. Large groups of women marched to demand equal rights. By the afternoon, women cloth workers, on strike in protest against bread shortages, were marching too. Other groups of strikers joined them. What was unusual about these demonstrations, and those of the next few days, was that the police and troops could not stop them. People went home as night fell. The next day, about 150,000 workers took to the streets armed with tools and metal bars. They seized food from the well-off areas of the city and held a mass protest. Demonstrations spread as the day went on, about everything from working hours to the lack of bread. The army and police were helpless, and the demonstrators were encouraged to further action. The leaders no longer needed to hide their faces from the police. Skilled workers, shopkeepers and office workers began to join them.

The Tsar makes things worse

On Saturday 25 February, hardly anyone in Petrograd went to work. About 200,000 took to the streets. There were red flags and banners saying 'Down with the Tsar' and 'Down with the War'. Some groups clashed with the soldiers; others tried to win them over. The troops had not yet fired on demonstrators, as they did in the 1905 Revolution. Then a telegram arrived from the Tsar. He ordered the general in charge of the troops in Petrograd to 'put down the disorders by tomorrow'.

> A young girl came out of the crowd of demonstrators and walked slowly towards the troops. Everyone watched in nervous silence: surely they would not fire at her? The girl took a bunch of red roses from under her cloak and held it out to the officer in charge. The red rose was a symbol both of peace and of the revolution. There was a pause. Then, leaning down from his horse, the officer smiled and took the roses.

Source A: *from* A People's Tragedy, *a history of the Russian Revolution written by Orlando Figes in 1996.*

> On February 27, Rodzianko, president of the Duma, sent a telegram to the Tsar. He told the Tsar that civil war had begun and was spreading, that the government was powerless, and that the Duma should be re-called. He ended his appeal with these dramatic words: 'The hour has come which will decide your fate and that of our country. Tomorrow it may be too late.'

Source B: *from* Imperial Russia, *a history of Russia before the Revolution, written by James Cracraft in 1994.*

examzone

Watch out!

The February Revolution is also called the March Revolution. This is because the Russian calendar was 13 days behind that of the rest of Europe. So 23 February–2 March in Russia was 8–15 March in Europe.

The army decides

The next day, 26 February, troops were ordered to fire at the demonstrators. This was a turning point. Some soldiers refused to fire and changed sides. Others fired, but the following day, 27 February, they refused their commanding officer's order to leave the Petrograd barracks. They ended up shooting him, then called on other troops to join them and took guns and ammunition with them to join the people.

Unrest turned into revolution. The Tsar and his government weren't ready for it, nor was the Duma. Even the Bolsheviks, Mensheviks and soviet organisers who had been talking of revolution, were startled by its sudden appearance. The army brought weapons to the revolution and organised the workers. Soldiers and workers fought together to capture the main weapons store, where they got hold of 40,000 rifles and 30,000 revolvers. They then went on to capture nearby weapons factories, taking more weapons. They fought the police, who had largely stayed loyal to the government. On 27–28 February they stormed the prisons, releasing the political prisoners. Now the Duma had to choose: should they support the Tsar or the revolution?

Source C : *protestors (the banner at the front is demanding an 8-hour working day) and troops in Petrograd in the tense days before the February Revolution.*

Activities

1 Use the text to make a timeline with a brief summary of the events from 23–28 February 1917.

2 Chose two of the adjectives below to describe the February Revolution. Write a paragraph to explain your choices.

frenzied   well-planned spontaneous   sudden effective   uncontrolled

3 What can you learn about the days leading up to 27 February from Source A?

A new government

News of the revolution was spreading. In Moscow workers and soldiers rose too, and other cities followed. But the revolution needed leadership. By the afternoon of 27 February, a large crowd was in front of the Tauride Palace, where the Duma met, yelling 'We need leaders! Give us leaders!' The Duma had a chance to take control. They met in one part of the Palace, while the **Petrograd Soviet** met for the first time since 1905 in another part.

While the others hesitated, 12 Duma deputies agreed with the Petrograd Soviet, on 2 March, that they would set up a **Provisional Government**, to run things 'unofficially' until a new government system was worked out and elections held. This government would have the support of the powerful Petrograd Soviet, as long as it worked to eight principles of government. These were:

1   Political prisoners and exiles to be freed from prison or allowed to return to Russia
2   Freedom of speech, of the press and to hold meetings
3   No class, religious or nationality discrimination
4   Preparations to be started for electing a **Constituent Assembly** to write a constitution
5   All police organisations to be replaced by an elected people's militia
6   Local government to be elected
7   Military units that took part in the revolution should not be disbanded or sent to the front to fight
8   Off-duty soldiers to have the same rights as civilians.

The Petrograd Soviet issued Order No 1 to the army in Petrograd. It said the army must obey the Provisional Government, 'except where the orders contradict those of the Petrograd Soviet.'

The Tsar abdicates

Meanwhile, the Tsar was finally returning to Petrograd – too late. His train stopped about 145 km from St Petersburg; the next station was held by revolutionaries. The Tsar's ministers saw that he and his wife were so unpopular that it would not be enough to offer to work with the Duma again. They suggested the Tsar should **abdicate**. At the same time as the Provisional Government was announced in Petrograd, the Tsar abdicated in favour of his brother, Michael. While the Duma considered this, the crowds took to the streets, chanting 'Down with the Romanovs' and 'Long Live the Republic'. Michael refused the crown and accepted the authority of the Provisional Government. Nicholas was taken prisoner.

examzone
Build better answers

Exam-style question: Explain why the February Revolution succeeded.

(8 marks)

The examination will always have questions on *why things happened* – like this one.

■   **A basic answer (level 1)** would give one or two reasons why the revolution succeeded, without any information to support them.

●   **A good answer (level 2)** would give detailed information to illustrate each reason. (For example: *... the army joined the people, bringing weapons and ammunition, and organised them.*)

▲   **A better answer (level 3)** would explain why each reason was important. (For example: *... the army went over to the people, taking weapons and organised them. Before that, people were not really having an organised revolution; just angry demonstrations against the government.*)

▲   **An excellent answer (full marks)** would show links between reasons. (For example: *... the suddenness of it, and the way the Tsar made it worse by telling troops to fire, were important. But the reaction of the army tied it all together. The army fired on people, but then went over to the people, taking weapons and organised them. Before that, it was angry demonstrations against the government rather than revolution. And the army then became an important part of the Petrograd Soviet and getting the Provisional Government accepted.*)

16

The main aim of both groups in the Palace [the Provisional Government and the Petrograd Soviet] was to restore order in the streets. There was a danger of the revolution falling apart. Thousands of drunken soldiers and workers were roaming the city looting shops, breaking into houses, beating up and robbing people in the street.

Source D: *from* A People's Tragedy, *a history of the Russian Revolution written by Orlando Figes in 1996.*

Source E: *soldiers of the Petrograd Soviet, meeting in the Duma building in March 1917. Look closely and you can see that some are wearing medals, while others are wounded.*

Activities

1 In pairs, write a different level 2 and level 3 answer for the question in the Build better answers box.

2 Write a sentence to explain why the army's reaction to the revolution was important to:

- the Tsar
- the demonstrators
- the Provisional Government.

Know Zone
Unit 2B - Key Topic 1

In the Unit 2 exam, you will have to answer six questions: Question 1(a), (b), (c) and (d); either Question 2(a) or Question 2(b); and either Question 3(a) or Question 3(b).

You only have an hour and 15 minutes to answer these questions. Use the number of marks available for each question to help you judge how long to spend on each answer. Remember to leave a few minutes at the end to check your spelling, punctuation and grammar in your answer to question 3. Here we are going to look at questions 1(a) and 1(b). Allow about 6 minutes for 1(a) and 7 minutes for 1(b).

Build better answers

Question 1 (a):

Tip: Part (a) questions will ask you to make an inference from a source and provide evidence from the source to support it.

Let's look at an example. Look at Source C on page 12.

What can we learn from this source about the Russian army in 1917? (4 marks)

Student answer	Comments
This source tells me that the army was ill-equipped, and ill-treated and that 1.8million soldiers had been killed and 3.9 million wounded.	This answer merely repeats information contained in the source. A good answer needs an inference (a judgement which is not actually stated in the source).

Let's rewrite the answer with that additional detail. The inferences are in bold.

This source tells me that the army was **a real threat to the government and likely to support a revolution because it was** ill-equipped, and ill-treated and that 1.8million soldiers had been killed and 3.9 million wounded.	There is an inference, supported by reference back to the source, making it a better answer.

examzone
Build better answers

Question 1 (b):

Tip: Part (b) questions will ask you to explain the key features of an important event or policy. Sometimes the words 'key features' will actually appear in the question. Or you could be asked about problems, or policies or effects. Don't just tell the story. Think about the information and organise it as if you were putting it under headings. This type of question requires you to write at greater length than in part (a) and is worth 6 marks. Let's look at an example.

Describe the key features of Russia under Tsar Nicholas II before the revolution of February 1917. (6 marks)

Student answer	Comments
One key feature was that the Tsar had all the power.	This answer gives only one key feature, and has added no detail.

Let's rewrite the answer to expand it and add detail.

One key feature was that the Tsar had all the power. Nicholas believed he alone should rule Russia and that he did not have to share power with the Duma (parliament). The Duma, set up after a revolution in 1905, was elected by only about 3% of the population, and had no power to make laws, but merely to advise the Tsar. Even that advisory power had seemed weak, particularly while the Tsar was away at war and the Tsarina seemed to draw more support from outside the Duma. A second key feature was the social inequality and prejudice against subject nationalities. About 125 million people lived in Russia, but just about 1 million owned all the land and wealth. Only about 55 million of the people actually spoke Russian but Russia dominated everything and the other nationalities in the Empire were squashed.	There are two developed features here.

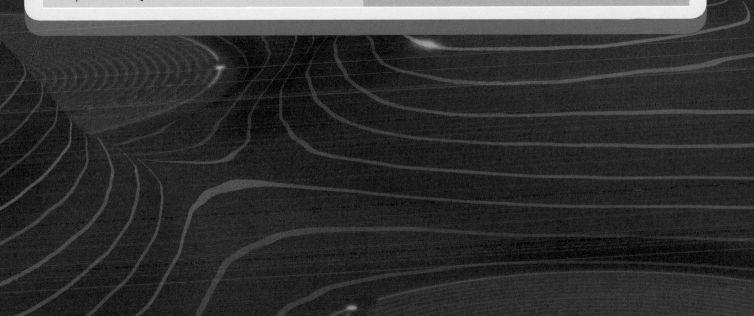

Key Topic 2: Bolshevik takeover and consolidation 1917–24

People had high expectations of the new Provisional Government. However, it did not make reforms quickly enough for many people, nor did it take Russia out of the First World War. It did legalise political parties and allow political exiles to return – but this meant people could be openly critical of its failings. The Petrograd Soviet, which had helped the Provisional Government to power, became impatient with its inaction, too.

In October 1917, there was another revolution. This time, the Bolsheviks, under Lenin, came to power. Unlike the Provisional Government, they acted quickly to take Russia out of the war and make reforms. But they were almost instantly swept into a civil war with various groups that wanted to control Russia. They won, but the country was in a terrible state. Industry and farming had suffered and people were starving. The Bolsheviks had to act fast, and accept political compromises, to improve the economy. By the time Lenin died in 1924, Russia's revolutions seemed to be over and the country had been reborn as the Soviet Union (USSR).

In this Key Topic you will study:

- the Provisional Government
- imposing Bolshevik control, 1917–21
- creating a new society, 1918–24.

The Provisional Government

Learning objectives

In this chapter you will learn about:

- people's hopes of the Provisional Government
- the Provisional Government's problems.

Activities

1 In pairs, make a list of what people hoped the Provisional Government would do. Put one colour tick next to anything that was fully achieved. Put another colour tick next to anything that was partially achieved.

2 In pairs, decide what the biggest problem the Provisional Government had to solve was: the war, shortages, or improving workers' conditions.

3 In pairs, decide what was the biggest weakness of the Provisional Government: control of the country, control of the army and the Petrograd Soviet, lack of decisive action, or political freedom for opponents.

High expectations

At first, the Provisional Government was popular, at least in places where people knew about the Revolution. Russia was so huge that in some places people had no idea what had happened. The new government gave political freedoms and promised a new Constituent Assembly, to be elected in November. People expected it would make reforms and rule effectively. Among the changes people hoped for were taking Russia out of the war, improving conditions for the workers in towns and cities and solving the shortages (especially of food and fuel). There were also many people who hoped it would redistribute property, especially land and farms, more equally.

Problems

The Provisional Government had problems giving people what they wanted. One problem was control. It needed the help of the Petrograd Soviet to get laws passed and acted on – the Soviet, not the government, controlled the workers and the army. The Provisional Government only controlled Petrograd and some cities and towns in northern Russia. Local landowners still controlled most of the countryside and would not have agreed to give their land away. Also, it saw itself as temporary, ruling until November's elections, and felt big changes should be made by the new, elected, government. It didn't pull Russia out of the war for this reason and because it felt it could not desert its allies. But the problems of supply and leadership were still there and the war went as badly as before. Other reforms, such as ending the shortages, needed time to take effect.

By April the government had:

- introduced an 8-hour working day
- made it legal for people to form political parties and hold public meetings
- released political prisoners.

These last reforms made it possible to criticise openly all the Provisional Government was failing to do.

Source A: *a Provisional Government propaganda truck in Moscow with the banner 'War to a Victorious End'.*

Bolshevik power grows

> ## Learning objectives
>
> In this chapter you will learn about:
> - the importance of Lenin
> - the growth of Bolshevik power
> - the effects of Kornilov's Revolt.

Lenin returns

Among the revolutionaries returning to Russia was Vladimir Ilyich Lenin, the Bolshevik leader. Lenin was an excellent speaker and a clear thinker. He held the Marxist view that **communism** could only come after a **bourgeois** revolution followed by a revolution of the workers. He was as surprised as anyone by the February Revolution. A few days before it broke out he made a speech saying the revolution might not come in his lifetime. It came.

On his journey back to Russia from exile, Lenin sent ahead a list of aims for the Party, the April Theses (see Source B). He said the Provisional Government was the result of the bourgeois revolution and that the Bolsheviks now had to work for the workers' revolution. It followed, then, that they should not co-operate with the Provisional Government, but work against it. He also stressed the need to get out of the war. On his arrival, he made a speech to the Petrograd Soviet, outlining his April Theses. The members were not impressed. Not many Bolsheviks agreed at first, either. But they came round to Lenin's view – especially when the first Provisional Government fell apart.

Bolshevik support grows

The first Provisional Government did not last. The second (5 May 1917) had members from all the main political groups except the Bolsheviks. Non-Bolshevik members of the Petrograd Soviet joined the Provisional Government, and still it did not take Russia out of the war or make reforms. The Bolsheviks gained a lot of support because the people of Petrograd, who had once regarded all revolutionary groups as similar, were now coming to see the Bolsheviks as the only real supporters of radical change and ending the war.

Source A: *Lenin (with umbrella) and some other Russian exiles, photographed in Stockholm on the way back to Russia in March 1917. They had to travel through a Europe at war.*

1   Withdraw from the war
2   Provisional Government is the bourgeois revolution that must happen before the workers' revolution; we must work for the workers' revolution
3   No co-operation with the Provisional Government
4   Work towards transferring power to the soviets
5   Work towards government by the people, not a parliament, with no police or central bureaucracy
6   All land to be owned by the state and run by the peasants on communal farms
7   All banks to become one state bank
8   Industry to be controlled by soviets
9   Party Congress to be called to change the Party Programme, mainly concerning the war, the need to demand a 'commune state'
10 A new International meeting (to agree these changes with Bolsheviks in all countries).

Source B: *The main points of Lenin's 'April Theses'.*

The Provisional Government had introduced bread rationing in March 1917. As the months passed, the amount of bread people could have fell. The war was still draining food and fuel supplies, and still tying up transport. In June 1917, Russian generals led another offensive. It failed, with more heavy losses. By the autumn, about 2 million soldiers had **deserted**. The Bolsheviks made the most of these difficulties. Lenin made inspiring speeches with simple slogans that the workers could remember, such as 'Peace, Land, Bread' and 'All Power to the Soviets'. He and Leon Trotsky gave strong leadership that united the Bolsheviks to spread their message. By June, there were 41 Bolshevik newspapers in the major cities criticising the Provisional Government and urging revolution. The Bolsheviks set up **Red Guards** of armed workers – by July there were 10,000 in Petrograd. Lenin's main problem was that the Provisional Government was so unpopular that workers might rise against it before the Bolsheviks were ready.

The 'July Days'

In July 1917, there was another unplanned rising in Petrograd. The people were reacting to the war, to bread rationing and to the Provisional Government's lack of reforms. The February Revolution had begun with groups demonstrating over different problems. The July rising was smaller, but now people were chanting Bolshevik slogans: 'Peace, Land, Bread' and 'More Power to the Soviets'. The Provisional Government acted like the Tsar – it sent in troops to clear the streets. Trotsky and several other Bolshevik leaders were arrested. Lenin escaped but had to go into hiding. Had the workers' revolution just failed?

Activities

1 Write *peace, bread* and *land* on separate cards. Write underneath each what the Provisional Government was doing about the issue.

2 Write a short speech for a Bolshevik about the event shown in Source C, explaining why it is so shocking.

3 Write a paragraph to explain why the Provisional Government failed to make more reforms.

examzone

Top tip

When asked to explain why something happened, a good answer should give at least three reasons, clearly explain why they lead to the outcome, and explain any links between them. So to answer 'Why was Lenin important in the rise of the Bolsheviks?', it would be true to say, *because he was an inspiring speaker*. It would be better to say, *because he saw they should not co-operate with the Provisional Government, and made inspiring speeches with memorable slogans like 'Peace, Land, Bread' which won lots of support in Petrograd.*

Source C:
a photograph of street fighting during the July Days.

The Third Provisional Government

Following the July Days, the Provisional Government again reformed, this time led by Alexander Kerensky, who had been in the government from the start as the only person who was a member of the Duma and the Petrograd Soviet. It took him three weeks to choose a government, asking people from the Petrograd Soviet and people from the old Duma. He chose Lavr Kornilov, a general known to be against the February Revolution, to command the army.

The new Provisional Government set out reforms of industry and land ownership to start before the November elections. This helped to slow the discontent among the workers, but made landowners and business owners unhappy. The Provisional Government's control in the cities still depended on the army. Meanwhile, in the countryside (where the Provisional Government had never had much control), the peasants began to rise up and take over land and food supplies from the landowners.

The Bolsheviks, meanwhile, carried on building support for opposition to the Provisional Government, while also warning of the danger of a **counter-revolution** by those who wanted to put the Tsar, at present a prisoner, back on the throne. The government was probably doing too little, too late, but it might have saved itself. However, on 28 August, Kornilov acted.

Kornilov's Revolt

Kornilov was disturbed by the growing unrest in towns and the risings in the countryside. He pushed Kerensky to impose **martial law** and break the power of the soviets. At first, Kerensky could not decide whether he wanted the support of Kornilov or the soviets – he could not have both. So he encouraged Kornilov to order his troops to advance on Petrograd, thinking they were saving the Provisional Government from the soviets. Then, claiming Kornilov was leading an army **coup** against the revolution, he armed the Bolshevik Red Guards (imprisoned in July) and sent them to stop him. Pro-soviet activists persuaded Kornilov's troops to stop their advance, so there was no fighting; but Kornilov and 7,000 followers were arrested. Kerensky presented himself as the saviour of the revolution – but his plan did not work. He became less popular, and people saw the Bolsheviks as the saviours of the revolution instead. They won most seats in the Petrograd Soviet election (31 August), whereas in April they had had none. Many workers now felt that the Bolsheviks, who had predicted a counter-revolutionary move, were the party of the people.

Food	July 1917	October 1917
fat	450g	96g
cheese	310g	91g
cabbage	310g	225g
sausage	500g	82g

Source D: *the rising cost of food in 1917. What you could get for 1 rouble.*

Month	Manual worker	Other
March	750g	500g
April	375g	375g
Sept.	250g	250g
Oct.	125g	125g

Source E: *the daily bread ration in 1917.*

It is now 13 days since the army ration was fixed at one pound of bread and less of hardtack [a 'biscuit' made from flour and water]. Since then, we have had less than half the flour needed to make this. The hardtack is almost all gone. Unless the front and the peasants nearby (who are starving) get food soon there will be terrible consequences.

Source F: *from a telegram sent by General Baluev at the front to the Provisional Government on 13 October 1917.*

Activity

Read the exam-style question in the Build better answers box. Write an exam-style question of the same type about the increased support for the Bolsheviks.

Source G: *some of the groups recruited by Kerensky to fight Kornilov's troops.*

Build better answers

Was the Provisional Government's failure to get out of the war the most important factor in its growing unpopularity? Explain your answer. **(16 marks)**
You may use the following in your answer:
- the war and its effects
- opposition groups.

You must also include information of your own.
This question is about *causation*.

■ **A basic answer (level 1)** makes a simple generalisation about causes.

● **A good answer (level 2)** agrees and/or disagrees with the proposition in the question but does not explain how other causes offered were causes (for example … *not getting out of the war was important, but it seems to me that the shortages of food and fuel were important too. And letting people speak out about their opposition will have had an effect on some people*). A more complete answer will examine more than two causes.

△ **A better answer (level 3)** will explain the causes discussed (for example, … *not getting out of the war was important, but it seems to me that the shortages of food and fuel were important, maybe even as important. Because people were starving, and you must feel your government should be changed if it can't stop you starving*).

△ **An excellent answer (level 4)** will prioritise the causes, or see links between them (for example, … *it was unpopular, basically, because it wasn't doing enough on many levels and many people had expected it to act. So it didn't take Russia out of the war. So the war was still draining people and resources and people were getting killed. It was harder to fix things like shortages when things were being diverted to the front all the time. Then, because it didn't have a tight enough control on the whole country it couldn't make social reform, like sharing out the land and all this inaction gave opposition groups a chance to criticise and turn people against it*).

The October Revolution

Learning objectives

In this chapter you will learn about:
- the events of the October Revolution
- the roles of Lenin and Trotsky
- the reasons for the Bolsheviks' success.

Lenin in exile

The Petrograd Soviet wanted to demand that the Provisional Government hand over power to the Congress of Soviets when it met on 25 October. Lenin, in exile in Finland, knew he had to act before then if he wanted a Bolshevik revolution.

Trotsky in Petrograd

On 8 October, Trotsky became chairman of the Petrograd Soviet, which now had a Bolshevik majority. He also ran its Military Revolutionary Committee. So the Bolsheviks controlled the most powerful group in Petrograd, while violence in the cities escalated. The Provisional Government, unable to keep control, even sent in the troops that remained in Petrograd against its own people. On 22 October, the generals at the front sent Kerensky a telegram saying, 'there is nothing to do but give up.'

The Bolsheviks take control

By 10 October Lenin had secretly returned to Petrograd. Rumours spread that he was back and planning a revolution, starting by taking over Petrograd. Kerensky did nothing. Between 24 and 26 October, following a plan worked out by Trotsky, the Bolsheviks took Petrograd. Lenin announced the Constituent Assembly election would still be held in November. Until then, a new **Council of People's Commissars** (CPC) would rule by **decree**. The Congress of Soviets elected a new group, the **Central Executive Committee** (CEC), to check the power of the CPC. Both groups had Bolshevik majorities. Trotsky had timed events to happen when the Congress of Soviets from many parts of Russia was meeting. Those who objected to the Bolshevik takeover walked out. The remaining members approved the changes so many people throughout Russia thought the whole Congress had approved them.

Timetable of Revolution

October 21 most army units in Petrograd promise loyalty to Trotsky and the Military Revolutionary Committee (MRC).

October 23 soldiers in Petrograd fort join MRC.

October 24 (night) Kerensky shuts Bolshevik news offices and orders the arrest of the MRC. The MRC take over the offices, the main river and canal bridges, the army headquarters and the telegraph station.

October 25 Congress of Soviets disagrees. Those against a Bolshevik takeover walk out. MRC takes over railway stations, post offices, the state bank and last 2 bridges over the river. Its troops besiege the Winter Palace (where Provisional Government meets).

October 26, 2.10 am the Winter Palace is captured and the Provisional Government is arrested. A new, Bolshevik, government is announced.

Source A: *a painting, from about 1923, of Lenin announcing the success of the revolution on 26 October.*

Why did the Bolsheviks win?

The Bolsheviks succeeded for several reasons.

- Lenin pressed the Bolsheviks to lead a revolution in October, and insisted it had to be Bolshevik, not one where several revolutionary parties ended up sharing power.

- The Provisional Government failed to disarm and disband the Red Guard after arming them to deal with Kornilov's Revolt (see page 20).
- The Provisional Government did not act against the threat in time. It completely misjudged the danger. Rumours of a revolt to overthrow the government had been in the air ever since the July Days – maybe it thought this threat was no more real than earlier ones.
- The takeover was well planned and organised by Trotsky. He organised the Red Guard and volunteers from the army, the navy and the factories to work together to a careful plan. There were times of confusion and disorder, but the main lines of the plan were carried out.

The plan included taking over the telephone and telegraph offices and the railway stations, making it hard for the Provisional Government to send for help. On 25 October, when the Provisional Government was besieged in the Winter Palace, Kerensky had to take a car and drive towards the front to look for help.

The Provisional Government had little support, so when it tried to gather troops in the city at the last moment, it found the MRC had persuaded most of the soldiers to join them or, at least, not to help the government.

In contrast to the Provisional Government the Bolsheviks provided the decisive leadership that people had been looking for since the revolution broke out.

examzone
Build better answers

Was Lenin's leadership the most important factor in the success of the October Revolution? Explain your answer.

(16 marks)

You may use the following in your answer:
- Lenin's leadership
- the actions of the Provisional Government.

You must also include information of your own.

■ **A basic answer (level 1)** makes a simple generalisation about causes.

● **A good answer (level 2)** agrees and/or disagrees with the proposition in the question but does not explain how other causes offered were causes. A more complete answer will examine more than two causes.

▲ **A better answer (level 3)** explains the causes discussed (for example, … *Lenin saw the need to act quickly was important. But Trotsky planned the takeover of key places stopping the Provisional Government from sending for help, giving the revolution time to establish itself.*).

▲ **An excellent answer (level 4)** prioritises the causes, or sees links between them (for example, … *Lenin saw the need to act fast, and timing was vital; but so was planning. Trotsky did that. Their control of the communication systems made it hard for the Provisional Government to get help. But if the Provisional Government had acted on the rumours, it might have stopped the revolution.*).

Make sure you write carefully – there are 4 extra marks available for spelling punctuation and grammar in these questions.

Activities

1 a Use the reasons below to draw a spider diagram of why the October Revolution succeeded. Add at least two more reasons from your own knowledge. Underline reasons to do with mistakes made by the Provisional Government in one colour and those to do with Bolshevik actions in another colour.

 b Draw lines to join reasons that are linked or set each other off.

- The Provisional Government made no social reforms.
- The Provisional Government freed and armed the Red Guard, then didn't disband it.
- The Provisional Government allowed political parties and free speech.
- The MRC won army support before October 1917.

Imposing Bolshevik control

28

The early decrees

On 25 October, Lenin (as chairman of the CPC) said the elections for the Constituent Assembly were to go ahead on 12 November. The CPC also passed some important decrees at once.

- **Capital punishment** was abolished.
- In towns and in the countryside power was given to the local soviets.
- *The Peace Decree* called on all nations to negotiate for peace at once. Russia began negotiating. Lenin was determined to get Russia out of the war at any price, for two reasons. Firstly, failure to end the war had undermined the Provisional Government, and it was also what the Bolsheviks had promised. Secondly, he feared a **civil war** might break out and wanted all Bolshevik troops free to fight that.
- *The Land Decree* took all land owned by the Tsar, other landowners and the Church, and gave it to the peasants, to be run by land committees. This only made what many peasants were already doing official, but it did make the Bolsheviks more popular with the peasants, who usually supported the Social Revolutionaries.
- *The Workers' Decree*, announced by the CPC three days later, gave the workers control over the factories and set an 8-hour working day.

The decrees met many of the demands of the people, but were not easy to enforce. As Lenin had feared, there were counter-revolutionary attacks in Petrograd and the other cities almost at once. Trotsky wanted to work with the other revolutionary groups, especially the Social Revolutionaries, who had a lot of support. Lenin wanted the Bolsheviks to have complete control. Despite the unrest and confusion, the Bolsheviks were still in power for the 12 November election. The results were a shock to them.

Leaving the war

Trotsky had the job of negotiating peace with Germany. The Germans, knowing Lenin was desperate to be free of this war to concentrate on the civil war in Russia, set a high price. Trotsky and others argued against accepting the terms, but, as the German army continued to advance, Lenin insisted. In the Treaty of Brest-Litovsk, signed on 3 March 1918, Russia lost: 80% of its coalmines; 50% of its industry; 26% of its railways; 26% of its people and 27% of its farmland – including the wheat-growing areas of the Ukraine. The treaty made many Russians, including many Bolsheviks, furious. But Lenin knew that the revolution would fail altogether if it had to fight both Germany and a civil war.

Party	Number of votes	Number of deputies
Socialist Revolutionary Party	17,490,000	370
Bolsheviks	9,844,000	175
Constitutional Democratic Party (Kadets)	2,000,000	17
Mensheviks	1,248,000	16
All other parties	11,118,000	120

Source A: *voting results from the Constituent Assembly elections, 12 November 1917. About 50% of all those who could vote voted.*

examzone
Top tip

It is important to get the *chronology* right – the order in which things happen. It may help to make a simple note like this:

25 October 1917: Bolsheviks take power.

12 November: Elections for the Constituent Assembly (to decide on a new constitution).

22 December: Treaty of Brest-Litovsk signed – Russia out of the First World War.

5 January 1918: Constituent Assembly first meet – only 25% of members are Bolsheviks. Lenin uses the Red Guard to end the meeting.

6 January: Red Guard stop any further meeting of the Constituent Assembly.

The Constituent Assembly

The Constituent Assembly, so long coming, met once, on 5 January 1918. The Social Revolutionaries and other groups argued against Bolshevik reforms that had been put in place by decrees, and would not pass them as laws. They were critical of the terms that the Bolsheviks were willing to accept with the Germans. Lenin brought in the Red Guard to shut the meeting down. The next day, those who arrived hoping to meet were sent away by the Red Guard. Lenin and the CPC were now running the country. But they had made themselves a great many enemies.

Red Terror

As the year went on, Lenin's speeches referred more often for the need for 'terror' during war and revolution. In September 1918 the CPC issued the decree 'Concerning the Red Terror', allowing a secret police (the **Cheka**) to send 'class enemies' to prison camps and shoot those involved in 'counter-revolutionary activities'. In other words, it could act against enemies of the Bolsheviks in much the same way as the Okhrana had acted against enemies of the Tsar. Some people criticised the decree, but Lenin and Trotsky spoke firmly in its favour. In November 1918 Trotsky said critics told him the terror was 'too harsh, too devoid of mercy', but concluded that Bolshevik survival depended on the Red Terror, for the moment.

Activities

1 Copy and complete the table below, covering each of the early decrees and the Treaty of Brest-Litovsk.

Decree	Details	Contrast to Prov. Govt.	Groups it appealed to and why	Why Lenin wanted it

2 Produce a PowerPoint presentation to tell the story of the Constituent Assembly from the decision to hold elections through to when the Red Guards turned members away on 6 January 1918. Find ways to display some of the information graphically, like a timeline and a pie chart.

Тов. Ленин ОЧИЩАЕТ землю от нечисти.

Source B: a Bolshevik poster from 1920. It says, 'Comrade Lenin cleans the world of rubbish', and shows him sweeping rulers, a priest and a capitalist away.

The civil war

> ## Learning objectives
>
> In this chapter you will learn about:
> - the events of the civil war
> - the effects of the civil war.

Reasons for the civil war

Civil war broke out in Russia in the winter of 1917. Many different groups took part, for different reasons. Some rulers of distant parts of Russia tried to seize land for themselves but the main opponents were the Bolsheviks (known as the Reds) and the Whites, an alliance of groups who wanted to get rid the Bolsheviks for different reasons. The largest White groups were:

- Kerensky and troops he raised, after fleeing Petrograd on 25 October, to restore the Provisional Government.
- Kornilov, Denikin and their Volunteer Army (mostly officers, some badly trained troops), monarchists fighting for the Tsar.
- Troops from the Allies (Britain, France, Japan and the USA) who were angry at Russia's withdrawal from the war and who were also against communism.
- Troops led by Kolchak, an ex-naval commander, with a capital at Omsk, in Siberia.
- The Czech Legion: about 40,000 Czech soldiers, once part of the Tsar's army, who refused to give the Bolsheviks their weapons, captured the Trans-Siberian Railroad and joined the Whites.

A new army

On 28 January 1918, Trotsky, the People's Commissar for War, called for volunteers to change the Red Guard into the **Red Army**. He ran the war, while Lenin ran the political changes. At first, the Whites had more supplies, troops and money than the Red Army. Foreign help meant that, from early 1919, they could attack the Bolsheviks from all sides (see map).

It soon became clear that the Red Army needed more soldiers and more discipline. Trotsky began conscripting soldiers and used officers who had served under the Tsar to train them. He held some families hostage, to make sure the officers stayed loyal to the Red Army. Most units had a **political commissar**, as well as an officer in charge. The political commissar was in charge of making sure the troops were educated in Bolshevik ideas. He also reported any disloyalty among the troops.

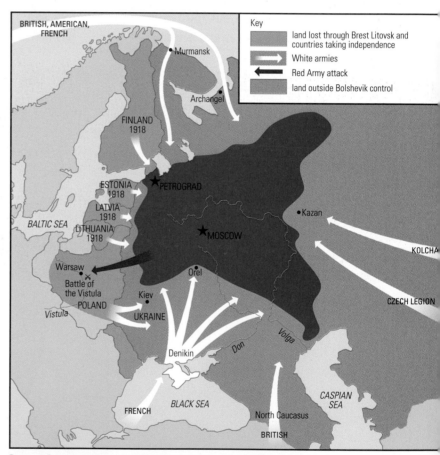

Source A: *pressure on the Bolsheviks during the civil war.*

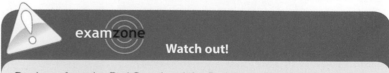

examzone

Watch out!

Don't confuse the Red Guard and the Red Army. The Red Guard were the workers' fighting units set up by the Bolsheviks, which never numbered more than 10,000. They had weapons and some training, but were not a proper army. The Red Army, set up on 28 January 1918 and run by Trotsky, was based on the Red Guard, but grew rapidly. In 1920, it had about 5 million trained soldiers.

Source B: Lenin speaking to Red Army troops about to leave to fight in Poland on 5 May 1920. Kamenev and Trotsky stand on the steps.

Main events of the civil war

In early March 1918, the Bolsheviks moved the capital to Moscow, which was more central, safer from attack, and had better communications. All through 1918 and most of 1919, the Whites advanced on Moscow and seemed certain to win. On 14 October 1919, Denikin's army was at Orel, just 300 km from Moscow and Kolchak was closing in. On 22 October, White armies were on the outskirts of Petrograd. This was the point of greatest danger.

Trotsky rushed to Petrograd and organised a counter attack, fighting with what the White leader called 'heroic madness' to drive them back. In early November 1919, the Allies gave up sending men and supplies, because they had decided the Whites could not win. The Whites found themselves spread thinly over a large area with fewer men and with supplies rapidly running out. Their troops began to desert to the Red Army. The Czech Legion went home, handing over Kolchak, whom they had captured, to the Red Army on the way. He was executed on 7 February 1920. In April 1920, the Red Army drove a Polish attack back into Poland and tried to start a communist revolution there. It failed. But by this point, the Bolsheviks had won the civil war. Various White groups kept on fighting into 1921, but they were no longer a serious threat.

Exam-style question

Describe the different opponents of the Bolsheviks in the Civil War.
(6 marks)

Activities

1 Use the information on pages 30–31 to make a timetable of the civil war, like the timetable box on page 26.

2 Turn this timetable into a graph of how well the Bolsheviks were doing in the civil war, with doing well at the top of the graph and doing badly at the bottom.

Bolshevik response to the war

The Bolsheviks responded to the problems created by the war by:

- enlarging the Red Army
- continuing the Cheka's Red Terror against political opponents – 'official' figures at the end of 1918 said there had been 6,300 executions; historians trying to estimate the real numbers give varying figures, but most estimate hundreds of thousands for the civil war years alone.
- introducing **War Communism** – taking control of all food and distributing it (with the Red Army coming first) and taking over all factories with more than ten workers (to control war supplies).

If it had not been for the war, the Bolsheviks would have introduced communism more steadily and been much less obvious in their use of the Cheka.

Why did the Bolsheviks win?

At the start of the war, no one expected the Bolsheviks to win. They won because:

- War Communism supplied the Red Army as efficiently as possible under the circumstances, although they were still short of supplies.
- unlike the Provisional Government, the Bolsheviks clamped down on resistance to the state – the Cheka made open resistance difficult and dangerous.
- Trotsky was a good Red Army leader. He went by special armoured train to speak to troops in the most dangerous places.

- Trotsky made inspiring speeches, gave out tobacco and other luxuries and even put on entertainments. On the other hand he executed leader of units, and sometimes their men, if he suspected disloyalty.
- The political commissar in each unit made sure the troops believed in the Bolshevik ideas they were fighting for.
- The Red Army had a military advantage called 'interior lines' – they were at the centre and so Trotsky could move men, for example, from Orel to Kazan much quicker than the Whites (who had to go all the way around) could.
- The Whites' only shared aim was to get rid of the Bolsheviks. They did not work well together, arguing over plans and leadership.
- The Whites had many officers, but had trouble getting enough soldiers. They had to conscript peasants, who did not really want the old regime of the Tsar back again.
- The Whites did not treat their troops well. When they began to lose, many of their units deserted and joined the Red Army.
- The end of the First World War, and the loss of foreign troops and supplies (as well as the Czech Legion) was a huge blow to the Whites. With the war over, the Western powers had no need for the Whites to get Russia back fighting Germany again.

Source C: *Trotsky speaking to members of the Red Army in 1920. You can see his train in the background.*

The effects of the civil war

At the end of the civil war, Russia was devastated. The country had been at war since 1914. The civil war had all the bad effects of the First World War – shortages of food and fuel, army casualties, loss of workers in towns. But war in Russia itself also:

- damaged land, property, road and rail links and telegraph lines
- caused civilian casualties
- meant skilled workers and professionals left the country to live somewhere safer.

Measures such as War Communism and the Red Terror lost the Bolsheviks support – they had not brought peace, land or bread. The civil war gave Bolshevik leaders their first experience of ruling. By the end of the war, they were used to ruling on military lines – giving orders and enforcing them, if necessary, violently.

Peasants reacted to having their crops and animals taken by hiding them and planting less. By 1920, the loss of farmland from Brest-Litovsk, the effects of war, and the reduced planting, meant crop production was only 37% of production in 1913. Prices had risen rapidly, money was almost worthless and most people were bartering (swapping) goods. Then, in 1920, drought hit. Crops dried up in the fields. People starved. Many people felt the civil war had brought this, too. It had certainly made things worse.

The shortages of food and fuel forced factories to close and workers were forced into the countryside to survive. Of the 3.5 million workers in factories before the war, only 1.5 were still working in factories in 1920. Moscow's population fell by half.

Source D: *from* The Soviet Experiments *written by R G Suny in 1998.*

Source E: *a Bolshevik poster from 1921 that reads, 'Remember the hungry!'*

Activities

1 Make a spider diagram, like the one you made on page 27, to show the reasons why the Bolsheviks won the civil war. Draw lines between factors that you think are connected.

2 In pairs, decide which factor was the most important in the Bolshevik victory. Think of three points to support your case.

3 Why did the Bolsheviks produce Source E?

Exam-style question

What does Source D tell us about the effects of the civil war in Russia? **(4 marks)**

Creating a new society

34

> ## Learning objectives
>
> In this chapter you will learn about:
> - the changes brought by communism
> - the effects of these changes.

The civil war pushed the Bolsheviks to try to turn Russia into the communist state they wanted as quickly as possible. They changed the name of the party from the Bolsheviks to the Communist Party in 1918. Russia became the Russian Socialist Federative Soviet Republic (the Russian Republic), which became the Soviet Union in 1922. Communism is based on social equality and shared wealth, so Lenin and the Bolsheviks wanted laws to make Russia more like this.

A new government

The Constitution of 10 July 1918 set out a new system of government. Local soviets elected deputies to regional soviets, which elected deputies to the Congress of Soviets. All workers could vote, those who made a living by the work of others could not (e.g. landlords). The Congress chose the Central Executive Committee (CEC), which chose the Council of People's Commissars (CPC): the people who ran the 18 Ministries that ran the country. The CPC made the laws, but the CEC and Congress of Soviets had to approve them. In December 1920, the Constitution was changed to let the CPC pass urgent laws without this approval.

A new society

The Constitution said all land, and all businesses with over ten workers (including banks), belonged to the state and must be run for the benefit of the people. It gave people the right of free speech, and a free press. It promised free education and medical care. All this was very different from the inequalities under the Tsar. However, the Constitution was the theory of how things ought to work. The civil war pushed the state to take measures that did not fit its beliefs. It imposed high levels of state control (in theory, it wanted to replace state rule with rule by the people). It wanted the workers to run factories, but ended up suppressing workers' committees and imposing state control. It used executions to control the country and the army (although it was against capital punishment in theory). It used the Cheka to control political opposition (see page 32) despite being in favour of free expression of political beliefs.

22. The Russian Republic, recognising the equal rights of all citizens, irrespective of their race or nationality, proclaims all privileges, as well as the oppression of national minorities, to be contrary to the laws of the Republic.

23. In the interest of the working class as a whole, the RSFSR can deprive all individuals and groups of rights they could use to the detriment of the socialist revolution.

Source A: *from the Constitution of 10 July 1918.*

Build better answers

Explain the effects of War Communism on Russia. **(8 marks)**

This is a question about *consequences*.

■ **A basic answer (level 1)** will make a general statement without any support.

● **A good answer (level 2)** will make a statement, and support it with some information.

▲ **An excellent answer (level 3)** will explain at least two effects, with supporting detail. (For example: *War Communism made food shortages in the towns and cities worse because the Red Army was always given priority for food and often there wasn't enough for the towns. Also the government was forced to clamp down on the workers – it took control of all factories that employed more than ten people, and outlawed strikes.*)

Source B: an anti-capitalism poster from 1919. The red slogans below read 'Either death to capital' and 'or death under the heel of capital.' The red banner says, 'Long live the power of workers' and peasants' soviets!' The black banner says, 'All power to the capitalists! Death to the workers and peasants!'

War Communism

War Communism, begun in May 1918, has been mentioned a number of times, so it is useful to bring it all together. It is the policy Lenin adopted to bring the economy completely under government control, to help win the civil war, and to destroy all opposition to communism. The main elements were:

- ending the market for food – peasants could not sell their crops, instead the state only left them a small amount for their own needs and took all the rest of their crops to distribute elsewhere
- assuming complete control of industry, which was directed only to make things needed for the war; strikes were banned
- having total control of the banks, and money and prices
- cutting back on people's rights – from banning strikes to using the Red Terror to destroy opposition.

Above all War Communism meant the needs of the army always came first. It did give the army the resources it needed, but at the terrible cost of extreme hardship.

Activities

1 In pairs, make a list of the ways War Communism changed the Russian economy.

2 Most people in Russia in 1919 could not read (about 70%) – so when they looked at Source B they would not know what the words said. Without using the information in the caption, what do you think somebody who could not read would understand by looking at Source B? Is it easier to work out by yourself, or talking to other people?

1921: a year of crisis

By the winter of 1920, the civil war was won. But Lenin continued with War Communism. In 1920, farm production was 37% of 1913 levels. Food shortages became famine. People were dying from starvation (in some areas cannibalism broke out). Industries were producing almost no consumer goods. There were riots in the countryside and strikes in the cities, especially Petrograd.

The Kronstadt Mutiny

Kronstadt was a naval base near Petrograd. The sailors there had sided with the revolutionaries of 1905 and 1917. In March 1921, horrified by the situation, and pushed over the edge by the way the Red Army crushed a strike in Petrograd, they **mutinied**, calling for 'a third revolution'. Their demands were:

- re-election of all soviets by **secret ballot**
- freedom of speech for workers, peasants, and revolutionary political parties
- freedom for all political prisoners
- ending the Red Terror
- free trade unions
- freedom for the peasants to farm as they wanted.

They saw themselves as being true to the revolutions of 1917. Red Army troops crushed the mutiny. The tenth Congress of Soviets was meeting at the time and, shaken, decided the policies of War Communism had to change. Lenin's answer was the New Economic Policy (NEP).

The NEP

The NEP was a step back from War Communism towards capitalism, taken reluctantly.

- Money was re-introduced, with a new coinage. Workers were paid wages again. There was a new state bank.
- The state stopped taking crops from the peasants. If they grew more food than they needed, they could sell it at a profit for themselves. But they had to pay the state 10% of that profit in tax, paid in crops.
- While the state kept control of the big industries, factories of under 20 workers could be privately owned and run to make a profit.
- The state brought in 'experts' to run the factories. Many came from other countries (between 1920 and 1925, 20,000 came from the US and Canada). Experts were paid more than workers. This was against communist theory, but they got the factories working again.
- Anyone could open a shop to sell or hire goods for a profit. These people became known as 'NEPmen'.

Year	Grain (millions of tons)	Coal (millions of tons)
1913	80.1	29.0
1920	46.1	8.7
1921	37.6	8.9
1922	50.3	9.5
1923	56.6	13.7
1924	51.4	16.1

Source C: *grain and coal production 1913–24.*

Year	Factory production (millions of roubles)
1913	10,251
1920	1,401
1921	2,004
1922	2,619
1923	4,005
1924	4,660

Source D: *factory production 1913–24.*

Exam-style question

Describe the key features of the NEP.
(6 marks)

Tip: Remember to give details to support your answer, for example: ... *they brought experts to run factories and make industry more efficient – 20,000 came from North America.*

Did the NEP work?

The NEP aimed to revive farming and industry. It seems to have done both.

- **Agricultural production** went up (see Source C). Statistics show that the peasants began sowing more crops – there were 77.7 million hectares of grain growing in 1922 and 98.1 million hectares in 1924. More families were keeping animals in 1924 than in 1922 as well; but in 1922 many families were recorded as having no animals because they had been taken for the war.

- Factory production went up, too. In June 1921, about 99% of all cotton mills were not working. By 1926, 90% were working again. However, factory production takes time to restart, and so the recovery was slower (see Source D). This led to a sharper rise in the price of manufactured goods than crops in 1923, but by 1924, as production increased, prices had begun to even out.

- The return to using money for wages and pricing of goods, as well as allowing small-scale profit-making seems to have built confidence, and more small-scale trading helped the economy.

Lenin dies

Lenin's health was poor from 1920 onwards. In May 1922, he had a stroke that left him partially paralysed. He dictated several documents to his wife after this, including his 'Testament' that expressed concern about divisions in the CPC. He had a second stroke in December, after which he stopped taking much part in politics. A third stroke, in March 1923 left him almost completely paralysed and unable to speak. He died on 21 January 1924.

Lenin was a hero to many Russians. His body lay in state in Moscow for the public to see for four days and nights. Nearly a million did so. His body was then embalmed and put in the Lenin Mausoleum in Moscow. Four days after his death Petrograd was renamed Leningrad in his honour.

Source E: *a poster produced in 1924 to celebrate Lenin's life and the part he played in the October Revolution.*

Activities

1 In pairs, make a list of the ways the NEP changed the Russian economy.

2 Read the following statements: *Lenin deserved to be seen as a hero by the Russian people. By the time he died their lives were better than in 1917.*

   Lenin did not deserve to be seen as a hero by the Russian people. 1920–21 shows how badly he let them down.

   In pairs, decide which of these statements you agree with most. List the evidence from this topic that supports your choice. Write your own statement summing up Lenin.

examzone

Top tip

When answering questions about change, be sure to give actual examples of before and after in your answer, for example: ... *under War Communism peasants were not allowed to sell their crops at a profit, under the NEP they could, as long as they paid the state 10% of that profit in crops.*

38

In the Unit 2 exam, you will have to answer six questions: Question 1(a), (b), (c) and (d); either Question 2(a) or Question 2(b); and either Question 3(a) or Question 3(b).

You only have an hour and 15 minutes to answer these questions. Use the number of marks available for each question to help you judge how long to spend on each answer. Remember to leave a few minutes at the end to check your spelling, punctuation and grammar in your answer to question 3. Here we are going to look at questions 1(c) and 1(d). Allow about 10–12 minutes for each of them.

examzone
Build better answers

Question 1 (c):

Tip: Part (c) questions will ask you to use your knowledge of the topic to explain effects or consequences. There are 8 marks for this question and you are required to go into things in a little more depth than you have done on parts (a) and (b).

Explain the effects of the October Revolution on Russia in 1917. (8 marks)

Student answer	Comments
One effect was that the Provisional Government was finished, Kerensky could not get troops to side with him because most of them had promised to support Trotsky and the Bolsheviks on October 23rd. In just a couple of days, the Bolsheviks were in power in Petrograd.	This answer is good about the fall of the Provisional Government, and the student has used accurate facts, like most troops agreeing to support the Bolsheviks before the revolution started. However, it only talks about one effect.

Let's rewrite the answer, adding information about the war.

One effect was that the Provisional Government was finished, Kerensky could not get troops to side with him because most of them had promised to support Trotsky and the Bolsheviks on October 23rd. In just a couple of days, the Bolsheviks were in power in Petrograd. **Another effect was to take Russia out of the war. Lenin's slogan had been 'Peace, Land, Bread' and he started negotiations with the Germans straight away. When the Germans pushed with harsh terms Lenin insisted that the Bolshevik government agreed to them to end Russia's part in the war. The Provisional Government believed in keeping Russia in the war, so this would not have happened without the fall of the Provisional Government.**	We now have a very good answer. It deals with more than one effect, and, in talking about how Russia would not have come out of the war if the Provisional Government had stayed in power, it shows us the way the effects were linked together.

Build better answers

Tip: Part (d) questions will ask you to use your knowledge to explain why something happened. In other words, this is a question about *causation*.

Let's look at an example.

Explain why the Bolsheviks were able to win the Civil War. (8 marks)

Student answer	Comments
Trotsky was a great commander and organiser, he moved to wherever the war was most difficult in his special train, and helped keep the Red Army confident. The Red Army was able to move troops about more easily than the Whites because of its interior lines. The Whites did not agree with each other, and didn't fight together. They also found it hard to get soldiers.	The candidate knows plenty of reasons, and has been able to support the answer with some good details — like Trotsky's train and the advantage of interior lines of communication. However, it is not explained why these reasons brought about the stated outcome (i.e. the Bolsheviks winning the war).

Let's rework the answer to put in some statements that pin the explanation to the outcome.
To help you, they are in bold.

The Bolsheviks won because of a mixture of their own strengths and the weaknesses of the Whites. Trotsky was a great commander and organiser, he moved to wherever the war was most difficult in his special train, and helped keep the Red Army confident. The Red Army was able to move troops about more easily than the Whites because of its interior lines. **So although they were being attacked by lots of different armies, they were usually able to get more troops to any place where there would be an important battle.** The Whites did not agree with each other, and didn't fight together. They also found it hard to get soldiers. **So they wasted their strength and made it easier for the Reds to beat them.**	Now we have the problems clearly linked to why the Bolsheviks won.

Key Topic 3: The nature of Stalin's dictatorship 1924–39

When Lenin died, in 1924, there was no clear replacement as leader. Many people assumed it would be Trotsky, but the person who emerged as leader was Stalin. Once in power, Stalin tightened his grip. Lenin had hoped **for a** worldwide revolution **where revolutions broke out in other countries to support the Soviet Union. Stalin saw the rest of the world as the enemy and concentrated on establishing 'Socialism in One Country'. He believed in a worldwide revolution, but later, and one led by a strong Soviet Union.**

It was not only outside the Soviet Union that Stalin saw enemies. He was increasingly concerned about opposition inside the Soviet Union. He used two existing Bolshevik policies. Firstly, he used propaganda and censorship to control people's understanding of what was going on. Secondly, he increased the terror begun during the civil war. The secret police arrested 'enemies of the state' individually or in groups. They held 'show trials' that always produced a 'guilty' verdict. The guilty were executed or sent to a system of prison camps run by an organisation called the 'Gulag'.

In this Key Topic you will study:

- the struggle for power 1924–28
- use of terror in the 1930s
- propaganda and censorship.

The leadership contest

Learning objectives

In this chapter you will learn about:

- Stalin's strengths and weaknesses
- the mistakes of his rivals
- how Stalin gradually removed his rivals.

Lenin had a stroke in May 1922, and another that December. After the second stroke he was not able to run the country or the Party. Worried about the future leadership of both, he dictated his *Political Testament* to his wife, telling her it had to be read at the Congress of Soviets after his death. After a third stroke in March 1923, he was bedridden and could not speak.

It seems clear from Lenin's *Testament* that he saw two main candidates for leadership of the Communist Party after his death – Trotsky and Stalin. It was their different characters and political views that he feared would split the Party. But Lenin did not think one person should dominate (even though he clearly did). So he did not name one person to take over. Instead, he assumed the whole Politburo, the committee that ran the Party, would take over. When Lenin died in 1924, there were seven Politburo members: Trotsky, Stalin, Rykov, Kamenev, Zinoviev, Bukharin and Tomsky. Of these, Trotsky, Stalin and Rykov were also in the CPC. In theory, they worked together. In fact, they competed for power.

Comrade Stalin, having become Secretary General, has gathered unlimited authority into his hands and I am not certain that he will always be able to use it with enough caution.
Comrade Trotsky is probably the most capable man on the Central Committee at present, but he is too self-confident.

Source A: *from the first part of Lenin's* Testament, *dictated to his wife after his first stroke in May 1922.*

Stalin is too rude and this defect becomes intolerable in the post of Secretary General. I suggest comrades think of a way of removing Stalin from that post and replacing him with a man who is tolerant, more loyal, more polite and more considerate to his comrades, less capricious.

Source B: *a postscript added to the end of Lenin's* Testament, *dictated to his wife ten days after the main part of the document.*

Activity

Use Sources A and B to complete the speech bubbles below.

Stalin's strengths and weaknesses

Stalin was probably the most ambitious member of the Politburo. His main political disagreement with Trotsky was that Trotsky, like Lenin, believed in world revolution. Stalin felt that the Soviet Union was so backward in agriculture and industry it would be attacked and destroyed by **capitalist** states, so the revolution had to happen at home first. Stalin believed in 'Socialism in One Country' – that the Soviet Union must modernise fast, to make it strong enough to protect itself from the capitalist countries of the West.

Stalin could be charming, but he had a quick temper. He was suspicious and, as Lenin said, given to sudden changes of mind for no good reason. Above all, he was clever and an excellent organiser and planner. He had been planning to take over from Lenin for some time. By 1922, he was a member of the Politburo and General Secretary of the Communist Party. He made sure his work kept him in Moscow, close to Lenin. He did all he could to seem Lenin's favourite and his job as General Secretary meant he chose who got jobs (in the Party and the government), so people wanted to please him to get and keep their jobs.

Trotsky's first mistake

Stalin knew he was not popular enough to take over the leadership on Lenin's death. He worked against his rivals gradually, building up his own power and support, and working to discredit them. Stalin began with Trotsky, his biggest rival. Stalin worked in Moscow, so he knew the other Politburo members well and most trusted him. They did not know Trotsky well, and some distrusted him because he seemed to be Lenin's favourite.

Stalin's first step was to stop Lenin's *Testament* being read to the Congress of Soviets. Kamenev and Zinoviev, supporters of Stalin, persuaded the rest of the Politburo not to sack Stalin as General Secretary or read the *Testament* to the Congress. Trotsky was not in Moscow when Lenin died. Some historians say Stalin gave Trotsky false information, so Trotsky missed Lenin's funeral. If he had hurried, he could have got back in time to lead the funeral march and give the funeral speech. Instead, Stalin did this. So many people felt he was the most important member of the Politburo – who else would do this important job? Recently, other historians have suggested Trotsky's lateness was not Stalin's fault. Stalin certainly benefitted from it.

Source C:
from the left: Stalin, Rykov, Kamenev, and Zinoviev, photographed in 1925.

Trotsky's removal

Immediately after Lenin's death, Trotsky, as a member of the Politburo, still seemed important. In fact, he was shut out of much decision-making. Stalin and his supporters spread an increasing number of rumours that Trotsky never really had Lenin's approval, that he disrupted the work of the Politburo and so on. Trotsky did not help himself by criticising Lenin and the NEP in a book in 1924. He lost jobs and power:

- **1925** resigned as Commissar of War
- **1926** was expelled from the Politburo
- **1927** was expelled from the Communist Party
- **1928** was exiled to Kazakhstan
- **1929** was exiled from the Soviet Union.

Removing other rivals

As soon as he was sure that Trotsky was losing support, Stalin began to move against his other rivals in the Politburo. He wanted to be the only leader, not one of a group. As Stalin got stronger, he could be more open in his attacks.

Even though they had worked with Stalin against Trotsky, Zinoviev and Kamenev were his next targets. During 1925 he made an alliance with Bukharin (earlier a supporter of Trotsky) and Rykov against them. Again, Stalin used rumours and accusations of disloyalty to the Communist Party. By 1926, the rivalry was out in the open. Kamenev and Zinoviev were driven into an alliance with Trotsky. Zinoviev was expelled from the Communist Party at the same time as Trotsky. Kamenev followed at the end of the year. By 1928, it had become clear that Stalin had replaced Lenin as leader of the Party and the USSR. Although there were still people who spoke out against him, they found it hard to get any support in the Party.

> Since Lenin's death, Stalin had rapidly been building up, through control of the Party's Secretariat [as General Secretary] a position of enormous power in the Party. His most serious rival, from the start of his rise to power in 1922, was Trotsky. To gain support against Trotsky, Stalin made an alliance with right-wingers in the party. He supported the policies of right and left in turn.

Source D: *from* The Government and Politics of the Soviet Union, *written by Leonard Schapiro in 1965.*

Activities

1 What can you learn from Source D about Stalin?

2 **a** In pairs, read the following answer to the question in the Build better answers box and decide what level it is.

> *Stalin got rid of opponents. He also managed to get a lot of his supporters into important jobs.*

b Now write a top level 3 version of that answer.

examzone

Build better answers

Explain how Stalin managed to overcome his rivals in power by 1929. **(8 marks)**
This question requires an *explanation of change*. It is not enough to describe the steps Stalin took, you will need to give details of the effects of the steps.

■ **A basic answer (level 1)** will give an example of a change, but without details. (For example: *He got rid of Trotsky.*)

● **A good answer (level 2)** will provide detail for the examples. (For example: ... *He got rid of Trotsky by making him less popular – making him miss Lenin's funeral, and working to have him lose his important jobs then get thrown out of the Communist Party.*)

▲ **A better answer (level 3)** will explain at least two steps. (For example: ...*There was getting rid of his rivals, by discrediting Trotsky and getting him and Kamenev and Zinoviev thrown out of the Politburo by 1927. But he also did it by putting himself in a powerful position as General Secretary of the Party, and having the power to give jobs and so on, so people supported him.*)

▲ **An excellent answer (top of level 3)** will link changes. (For example, adding to the above: ... *He would not have been able to get rid of his rivals as easily had he not worked his way into a position of power as Party Secretary.*)

Stalin's police state

Learning objectives

In this chapter you will learn about:

- the use of terror, especially the purges
- the work of the secret police
- the importance of show trials.

The Bolsheviks had kept power during the civil war by clamping down on political opposition using the Cheka and Red Terror (see page 29). After the war, Lenin still wanted to keep control, but the Cheka had a bad image. In 1922, it was reformed as the GPU (State Political Administration), then the OGPU (Unified State Political Administration). Well before Stalin took over, the key elements of control by terror were in place.

A state police

The OGPU dealt with political 'crimes' – opposition to the state. Local police forces still handled ordinary crimes, although, over time, more and more crimes became 'political'. It was just the Cheka under a different name, with many of the same people in it. The OGPU could arrest people and get confessions by many methods, including torture. It could imprison people in camps without trial, or organise trials where the verdict of 'guilty' was decided before they began. The Cheka had had, and used, all these powers. In addition, the OGPU could send people into any organisation or factory to look for evidence of **sabotage** by 'anti-communists'. The state often suspected such sabotage when problems were really the result of incompetence.

Prison camps

When the Cheka was set up, so were camps for political prisoners. The Cheka also had prisons in towns and cities, but the camps were isolated in the countryside, often in the north of the country. By the end of 1920, the Cheka had sent about 250,000 prisoners to such camps. The prisoners were used as cheap labour.

A climate of fear

What the Bolsheviks wanted during the civil war was for political opponents to be too scared to speak out. The Cheka's methods were intended to frighten – Lenin compared their activities to the 'Terror' of the French Revolution when many people were killed.

exam zone

Watch out!

Students often get confused by the different names of the secret police through this period:

Before the revolution the Okhrana
1917–22 the Cheka
1922–23 the GPU, part of the NKVD (which included the ordinary police and the prisons)
1923–34 the OGPU
1934–45 the GUGB, part of the NKVD

exam zone

Build better answers

What can we learn from Source A about the Politburo's attitude to the purges?

(4 marks)

This is an *inference* question. It asks you to work something out from the source.

■ **A basic answer (level 1)** will give information from the source. (For example: *They ordered local officials to arrest and shoot people.*)

● **A good answer (level 2)** will make an inference without supporting it from the source. (For example: *... they agreed with the policy.*)

▲ **An excellent answer (level 3)** will use details from the source to support that inference. (For example: *... they agreed with the policy because they ordered local officials to arrest and shoot people.*)

The terror under Stalin

Stalin expanded the powers of the OGPU and the scope of their activities. They encouraged people to inform on neighbours, friends, even family who spoke out against the state. By 1930, the system of labour camps had grown so much that the state needed a special department to run them all. In 1928, there were about 30,000 people in camps. By 1938, there were about 7 million. The department running them was called the *Gulag*, and the name was soon applied to the camps themselves.

The purges

By 1934, Stalin feared growing opposition to himself and the state. He began the 'Purges' – moves to destroy these enemies. Those purged were either executed, exiled to labour camps (the *Gulag*), or exiled abroad. Stalin had changed the way farming and industry were run in order to raise productivity. When there were failures, the state suspected sabotage by political opponents (rather than incompetence by officials), and used the purges to set things right. The purges were so harsh between 1936 and 1938 that these years are called the Great Terror: millions were purged.

The OGPU purged:

- the Politburo
- the Communist Party
- teachers
- engineers, scientists and industrial workers
- the armed forces
- even the secret police.

By 1939, Stalin had purged important Party leaders and people at a local level. Factories, schools and colleges were also purged of anyone thought to be 'enemies of the people'.

The Politburo did not even specify the names, but simply gave out death quotas by the thousands. On 2 July 1937, they ordered local officials to arrest and shoot 'the most hostile anti-Soviet' people, who were to be sentenced by the local Party Secretary, judge and NKVD chief.

Source A: *from* Stalin, *written by Simon Sebag Montefiore in 2003.*

Source B: *a French cartoon about Stalin's Russia, first printed in 1938. The words on the placard are, 'WE ARE REALLY HAPPY' but we can see that the man does not mean it, and only holds it because the soldier has a whip and a gun.*

Activities

1   **a**   In pairs make a bullet point list of the key features of the Terror under Stalin.

   b   Underline those that were already in place when he came to power.

2   List and explain the causes of the purges (you should have at least two).

A fair trial?

In 1934 Kirov, a Politburo member, was murdered, possibly on Stalin's orders, although Stalin claimed to be outraged. In 1936 show trials began. Sixteen 'Old Bolsheviks' (people who had been leaders of the revolution in 1917) were tried for treason and the assassination of Kirov. They confessed, although they were not guilty. The Chief Prosecutor concluded by saying, 'I demand that the mad dogs be shot! Every one of them should be shot.' They all were. The OGPU arrested 40,000 suspects for 'trial'. Each trial lasted just a few minutes; all were 'guilty'. Some were shot, others sent to the *gulag*. Eugenia Ginzburg, sent to the *gulag* for ten years, protested that Kirov was murdered in Leningrad, a city she had never been to. The judge replied, 'but Kirov was killed by people with your ideas, so you must share the responsibility.'

The importance of show trials

The trials were important because:

- Ordinary people did not know, at first, how unfair they were: the accused were reported as having had a trial.
- The accused usually confessed; this was also reported.
- The trials suggested to people that there was a danger to the revolution from inside the Soviet Union. It made them more likely to unite behind Stalin against it.
- The trials scared people and made them less likely to be critical.

By virtually wiping out the old generation of Communists (including every one of those close to Lenin before and after the revolution) and filling the party and state administration with newcomers who stepped into dead men's shoes and owed him everything, Stalin created loyal support for himself.

Source C: *from* Socialism in One Country, *written by Judith Bassett in 1978.*

examzone
Top tip

It is important to give as much detail as you can to support your answers in the examination. Good answers never just say 'x was a factor', they explain why and how it was a factor, using examples. Similarly, good answers never just say 'x was the most important reason'. They give several reasons, weigh them up against each other and then say which reason they think was the most important and why.

Source D: *this image of Lenin and eleven 'heroes' of 1917 was published in 1920. By the end of 1938, five had been executed, one was in the* gulag, *one was dead of natural causes, Trotsky was in exile, one had left to live in the USA in 1918 and two had been sent abroad as diplomats. None remained in government.*

Effects of the purges

The purges were supposed to clean out enemies of the state and produce a country where everyone was dedicated to working for the Soviet Union, or USSR as it was also called. After 1938, the purges slowed, but their effects remained. They:

- created an atmosphere of fear and suspicion: no one knew who to trust. This enforced obedience, but also gave rise to a lot of resentment.
- took away people's trust in the justice system
- killed about a million people
- sent about 7 million people to prison
- meant the state lost useful people at all levels, including 1 million of the 3 million members of the Party, 93 of the 139 Central Committee members, and 13 of the 15 top generals in the Red Army
- removed a lot of skilled workers from industry, so factory production was reduced
- produced a government and a Party almost totally created by Stalin and loyal to him. Experienced people had been replaced by Stalin's yes-men. The country, and especially the army, was weaker as a result.

Source E: *workers at the Stalin Factory in Leningrad vote to approve of the executions of the 'enemies of the people' in the first show trial in 1936.*

Did you know?

It is impossible to give accurate numbers of those purged. Secret Police records, only released in 1990, suggest that in 1939 there were 3,593,000 people imprisoned by the secret police – 1,360,000 were in the *gulag*. The figures for those shot have not been released. People disagree over interpreting the statistics we do have. For example, historians disagree about the percentage of Red Army officers purged (estimates range from 10% to 50%).

Activities

To complete these activities use all the material on pages 44–47.

1 **a** List and explain the key features of the purges (you should have at least four).

   b List and explain the consequences of the purges.

2 Find details to support the following generalisations (see page 11 for an example of how to answer this type of question).

   a Ever since the revolution Russian governments had relied on terror.

   b The purges affected many different parts of Russian life.

   c The show trials were not fair.

   d The purges and the Great Terror made Russia weaker.

Propaganda

> **Learning objectives**
>
> In this chapter you will learn about:
> - the use of propaganda
> - propaganda in education
> - the cult of Stalin.

Propaganda is giving information, true or false, to make people think or behave in a particular way. Stalin used propaganda:

- to turn people against his enemies
- to get people to accept his decisions (such as his changes in industry and agriculture)
- to get people to put up with hardships
- to get people to work harder
- to build up a 'cult of Stalin'.

Types of propaganda

Stalinist propaganda was everywhere. The state controlled the radio and the newspapers, so they had to produce Stalinist propaganda. People wrote propaganda songs, poems and books, too. The state used **censorship** (see pages 52–53) to make sure no publications said anything that was 'anti-Soviet', which meant anti-Stalin.

The government sent officials all over the USSR, with propaganda films and other material, to give talks in the towns and villages. They stressed how everyone had to work together for the USSR and Stalin. Banners and posters on buildings, in shop windows, even on trains and trams, spread different messages at different times through propaganda slogans. Each new policy like collectivisation or the Five-Year Plans (see pages 57 and 64), came with its own propaganda campaign. Stalin was regularly photographed with smiling children or workers, especially workers from the different regions of the USSR, to show how widely popular he was.

Foreign visitors to the Soviet Union had to travel under state supervision. Their state guides took them to factories, **collective** farms and homes of 'ordinary' people. They were, in fact, taken to 'show' places, designed to give the impression that workers had a far better life than they did.

Education

The Bolsheviks provided free education, intending to wipe out the high levels of illiteracy in the Soviet Union. While the quality of teaching varied, early schools focused on basic literacy and numeracy.

Under Stalin, schools became a place to spread propaganda. Textbooks, which had to be state approved, were full of propaganda. Teachers were purged if they did not teach the Stalinist view of the world. The Stalinist view, especially of history, often changed, as people fell out of favour with Stalin. When this happened, teachers gave out pots of paste and pieces of paper, and children pasted over the faces of those out of favour. Children were also encouraged to 'denounce' family and friends of the family who were anti-Stalinist, while the children of families suspected of being enemies of the state were often bullied.

> That contemptible enemy of the people, the fascist agent Trotsky, and his contemptible friends, Rykov and Bukharin, organised in the USSR gangs of murderers and spies. They foully murdered that committed Bolshevik, Kirov. They plotted to murder other leaders of the proletariat too. They caused train collisions, blew up and set fire to mines and factories, wrecked machines, poisoned workers and did all the damage they possibly could. Their plan was to restore the capitalists and landlords to the USSR, to surrender the Ukraine to the Germans and the Far East to the Japanese.

Source A: *from* A Short History of the USSR, *a school history textbook written by A V Shestakov in 1938.*

examzone
Top tip

When explaining how propaganda works, think about the language the writer is using. Is it pushing you to feel a particular way about what it is describing? Propaganda often uses emotional language. Photographs and cartoons do the same thing – for example, a photo making Stalin look loved or a cartoon making fun of Trotsky.

Propaganda was everywhere, including the media, the arts, and education. Its main messages were that life in the Soviet Union was unarguably better when contrasted with the pitiful lives of workers living under capitalists and landlords; that everyone in the USSR enjoyed satisfying jobs and high living standards, agreed with Party policy and was devoted to Stalin.

Source B: *from* Popular Opinion in Stalin's Russia, *written by SR Davies in 1997.*

Activities

1 a Turn the 'types of propaganda' section into a bullet point list.

b In pairs, draw up a table using the bullet points at the top of page 48 (the uses of propaganda) as headings for the rows.

Go through the entire book looking at the sources. Work out which were originally created as Stalinist propaganda and list them in the table under the particular use of propaganda they show.

2 a Copy out Source A, taking out all the emotional language.

b Is Source A an acceptable school textbook?

3 Source C is a photo of a travelling propaganda squad visiting a village to talk about the advantages of collective farms. Was it also made to be propaganda itself? Give reasons for your answer.

Source C: *a state official lecturing a group of peasants on the benefits of collectivisation, the method of farming that Stalin was forcing on the USSR. The poster reads 'These farm workers say go to the collectives.'*

The cult of Lenin

Stalin did his best to remove political competition and any early revolutionaries, with the exception of Lenin. Lenin was widely loved and respected before his death. After his death, Stalin did not try to discredit Lenin. Instead, he built up a cult of Lenin, making him even more important. This had the effect of making Stalin's image of himself as Lenin's chosen successor more acceptable, even to those who knew Lenin was closer to Trotsky.

The cult of Stalin

Stalin's supporters quickly began building a cult of Stalin. Many people took to it wholeheartedly. Stalin always said publicly that Lenin and the Soviet Union and its people were more important than he was. But Stalin was everywhere you looked in the Soviet Union. His face looked down on you from vast posters attached to the fronts of shops and blocks of flats. The papers carried photos of him every day, articles about how his reforms were making the country a better place, and how much people loved him. None of this could have happened without Stalin's approval. Ordinary people wrote to Stalin asking for help, sometimes he gave it. This made him even more popular.

Exam-style question

What can you learn about the 1936 Constitution from Source F?
(4 marks)

Tip: To answer this question you need to make an *inference*, work something out from what the source tells you. When making an inference from a source, be sure to use evidence from the source to back up your information. So, don't say, ... *it was used for propaganda.* Say, ... *it was used for propaganda, to make people praise Stalin and to make them think the state was approved of and democratic.*

Source D: *a 1936 poster that says: 'Long Live the People – the Great Stalin – the Constitution.'*

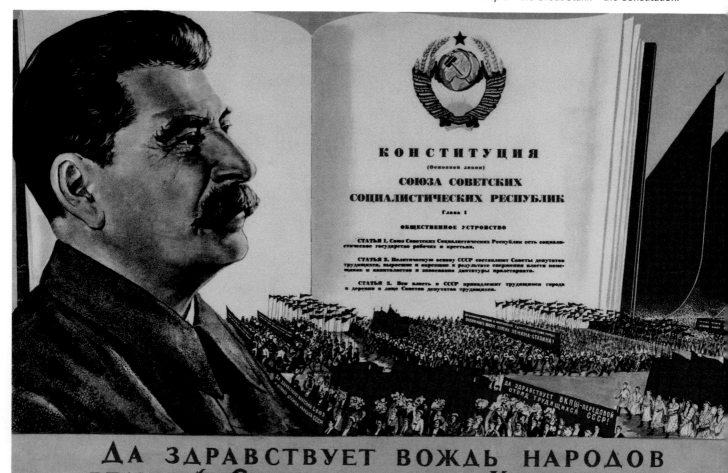

ДА ЗДРАВСТВУЕТ ВОЖДЬ НАРОДОВ
ВЕЛИКИЙ СТАЛИН — ТВОРЕЦ КОНСТИТУЦИИ
ПОБЕДИВШЕГО СОЦИАЛИЗМА И ПОДЛИННОГО ДЕМОКРАТИЗМА

The 1936 Constitution

In 1936 a new Constitution, 'Stalin's Constitution', was introduced, praised as 'the most democratic system in the world'. The democracy it set up was mostly an illusion – some historians have seen it as mostly propaganda. The Supreme Soviet, made up of the Soviet of the Union and the Soviet of Nationalities (for the republics that were part of the Soviet Union), now ran the country. Everyone could vote and voted directly for representatives. Everyone was guaranteed rights such as the right to work and the right to education and healthcare. The local laws of the 15 republics were to be as important as the 'national' laws from Moscow.

In practice, the Supreme Soviet met for only a few days each year. The Politburo still had the real power. There was only one party, the Communist Party. State-controlled officials chose all the candidates for elections – so people were bound to choose someone approved of by the state. Various guaranteed rights, including freedom from arrest without a proper trial, could be, and were, ignored 'in the interest of national security'.

51

Stalin was seen as having superhuman powers – 'taller than the Himalayas, wider than the ocean, brighter than the sun' (in the words of a poet). Stalin became the modern 'little father' to the great mass of Russian peasants – a term traditionally applied to the Tsars.

Source E: *from* Josef Stalin, *written by Helen Rappaport in 1999.*

The new Constitution was an excuse for more Stalin-worship (but any excuse was enough for this at that time in the USSR). It was also used to show the free and democratic nature of the Soviet regime both at home and abroad. The widespread approval of the draft version was used to show support for the regime. The one-party system, according to Stalin, ensured democracy for the working people.

Source F: *from* The Government and Politics of the Soviet Union, *written by Leonard Schapiro in 1965.*

Activities

1 How does the poster (Source D) work to support the cult of Stalin (give two pieces of evidence)?

2 Copy out the following democratic freedoms granted by the 1936 Constitution. Write below each one what happened in practice.

- everyone votes for a candidate for the Supreme Soviet
- laws of the Republics respected
- the Supreme Soviet ran the country
- people had many rights 'guaranteed' by the Constitution

3 Make a table like the one here, and fill in the three sections. Put a series of statements into each one and add some supporting detail.

Stalin's use of propaganda
Reasons why he used it
Key Features
Effects

Censorship

Learning objectives

In this chapter you will learn about:
- the use of censorship
- the creation of an official culture
- the effects of censorship.

Another way that Stalin controlled the information that people received was by censorship. Censorship is telling the media what they can or cannot print or say. Stalinist censors controlled what went into radio programmes and newspapers. But they had a far deeper effect, creating an official culture that was part of the propaganda system.

The official culture

Stalin wanted a culture of social realism – a culture available to everyone, that could be understood by everyone. He thought education was very important, but disapproved of 'high' (hard to understand) culture, which he said worked against equality. Writers, poets, artists and musicians had to produce 'low' work with a simple, patriotic, message. So what the censors were really doing was making culture part of the propaganda system. Writing a poem or a piece of music that did not fit in made you an 'enemy of the people'. Arrest and the *gulag* usually followed, unless you could find a way to get back into favour.

Stalin had his favourite painters, writers, poets and singers. He admired Gorky, Shostakovich and the singer Kozlovsky. He often invited people to give private performances or readings at the Kremlin, as well as private film screenings. But Stalin's favourites could fall into disfavour. Sergei Eisenstein was a cartoonist for a Bolshevik newspaper and worked in 'low' culture theatres in the 1920s. He turned to film-making. In 1925, he made *The Battleship Potemkin,* a film about the 1905 Revolution. It was very popular, and Stalin encouraged Eisenstein to make more films. Unfortunately, Eisenstein's next film, about the October Revolution, was censored because it referred to Trotsky. From 1928 to 1930, Eisenstein toured Europe and the USA, with official permission. The fact he had been to the West made many people suspicious of him, and the films he made on his return were criticised by the All Union Conference of Cinema Workers for being too 'high'. He had to go back to 'low' films, or risk becoming an enemy of the state. So he did.

Once, when Kozlovsky was performing at the Kremlin, different members of the Politburo began demanding different songs. 'Why put pressure on Comrade Kozlovsky?' Stalin intervened calmly. 'Let him sing what he wants.' He paused. 'And I think he wants to sing Lensky's aria from Onegin.' Everyone laughed and Kozlovsky obediently sang the aria.

Source A: *from* Stalin, *written by Simon Sebag Montefiore in 2004.*

Exam-style question

Explain why censorship was important to the Stalinist state. **(8 marks)**

 examzone
Top tip

Question 3 asks you to consider the relative importance of reasons, changes or effects. For example, it might suggest that one reason for an event was most important. It will then suggest two more reasons to consider and tell you that you must use information of your own in your answer. You must consider all three reasons in the question. If you can think of other reasons that you can support with detail, discuss them as well. Remember that this question is asking you to make a judgement, so remember to make your judgement (and your reasons for making it) clear once you have weighed up the various reasons.

Censoring the past

Stalin's censors edited the past all the time. They didn't just tell people what to say about the past. They also went to work on evidence from the past, removing or changing it. They destroyed many books, documents and photos. Other photos were censored by removing people who had fallen from favour with Stalin, or whose role in the revolution he wanted to play down (Trotsky, for example). In some famous photos, you can track the fall of people from favour through several versions of the photo, as they disappear in ones and twos.

Compared to some of the photo censoring, Source B has been carefully changed. In some cases, all the censor did was blot out the faces of people with black ink. In these cases the censorship acted as a warning about what happened to opponents.

1 Compare Source B with the photo on page 31 and work out who is missing. Write a paragraph to explain how this censorship of a photo would be useful to Stalin.

2 Read this possible question 3.

   Was censorship the main reason Stalin was able to stay in power in the USSR?

   In the exam you would be given censorship and three other things to consider. Make a list of at least three alternatives to censorship you could consider when answering this question.

Source B: *this version of the photo of Lenin talking to the troops in 1920 was always used after 1928.*

In the Unit 2 exam, you will have to answer six questions: Question 1(a), (b), (c) and (d); either Question 2(a) or Question 2(b); and either Question 3(a) or Question 3(b).

You only have an hour and 15 minutes to answer these questions. Use the number of marks available for each question to help you judge how long to spend on each answer. Remember to leave a few minutes at the end to check your spelling, punctuation and grammar in your answers to questions 2 and 3. Here we are going to look at questions 2(a) and (b). Allow about 12 minutes for this question. It is worth 8 marks, but there are also 3 additional marks available for spelling, punctuation and grammar.

examzone
Build better answers

Question 2 (a)

Tip: Question 2 will ask you to use your knowledge to explain how something changed or developed. In the examination you can choose to answer whichever of Question 2(a) or (b) you like the most. Do not do both (a) and (b) as you will only be awarded marks for one of them.

(a) Explain how Stalin was able to overcome his leadership rivals in the years 1924–28. (8 marks)

Student answer	Comments
It was quite simple, starlin got rid of his rivels until he was the only won left.	Oh dear. This isn't very good. It is true that Stalin got rid of his rivals, but the candidate hasn't explained • who the rivals were • the different ways he used to 'get rid of' some • how he dealt with the ones he didn't 'get rid of'. The spelling, punctuation and grammar are also poor.

Let's rewrite the answer with additional detail.

It was quite simple, Stalin got rid of his rivals until he was the only one left. **Trotsky was the first target. He gave him the wrong date for Lenin's funeral, so Trotsky didn't go, and Stalin spoke at the funeral. This made people think Stalin was closest to Lenin, so they were more likely to support Stalin.** <u>Stalin also used his power as Secretary of the Party to put people who supported him in important jobs in the party, rather than people who supported the other leaders. This meant support for Stalin grew, and support for the others got less.</u>	There is more that could be said here, but the candidate has now explained one way – how Stalin dealt with Trotsky. In the underlined section, the candidate goes on to *explain* how Stalin used his position as Party Secretary to weaken his leadership rivals. The spelling, punctuation and grammar are also much improved in this answer.

★ examzone

Build better answers

Question 2 (b)

Let us now look at Question 2 (b). This time, instead of looking at a student answer and examiner's comment, we will trace the thought processes of the student writing the answer. A suitable question would be:

(b) Explain how Stalin's methods of keeping control changed over the years 1924–38.

Student thought processes	Student answer
Why the dates 1924–38? That's from the death of Lenin to the end of the purges. What about 'internal security policies'? That means the different ways they kept control of the country. I'll start by saying he used lots of different methods. I don't suppose the marks are for that, though, so I'll keep it short.	After Lenin's death, Stalin used a number of different methods to keep control, including the secret police, propaganda, and then purges and show trials.
Now I need to talk about the different methods and how they changed. Must remember to put the dates in to show when it changed.	At first Stalin had to be quite careful. He just moved against Trotsky, getting the support of the other leaders against him. Trotsky was expelled from the party then exiled. By 1928, Stalin was in a strong position, and he started to be more extreme. He used the secret police to spy on people, and then sent terror squads into the countryside. In 1934, he began the purges in the Politburo, the Party, the army and even individual schools and factories. Lenin's secret police had sent some people to labour camps, but now millions were sent. In 1936, he started show trials when 16 old Bolsheviks were tried for treason and the murder of Kirov. They were all executed. Any criticism of Stalin could get you arrested.
Is there anything else I can add? Yes — I've got some changes — move against Trotsky, secret police, purges, show trials. Are there any links between them? I'll explain them.	Stalin's determination to be secure as the only leader links all these together – he got rid of Trotsky because Trotsky was his rival, then he was able to be more open in moves against others. In 1934, he thought opposition to him might be growing so he made things tougher with the purges – now that Trotsky was gone he could link people to Trotsky and purge them. The show trials made people more likely to accept the purges, because these famous Old Bolsheviks were pleading guilty, and it was in the papers and on the radio. He got rid of all the remaining Old Bolsheviks, so Stalin was the only leader of the 1917 revolution left.

Key Topic 4: Economic and social changes 1928–39

Stalin was convinced that the capitalist world would try to crush the communist Soviet Union. So he wanted to make the country strong by improving productivity in agriculture and by rapid industrialisation. His chosen method was state control and state ownership, with farms and factories run to meet production plans imposed by the state. By 1939, Stalin's plans had greatly increased productivity in farming and industry. The price was high, though: it included a widespread famine in 1934.

Was life in the Soviet Union better now than it had been under the Tsar? How had things changed? Had the Communist Party achieved its aim of an equal society? The answers to these questions depended on who you were and where you lived – and whether you were prepared to accept state propaganda and obey official orders.

In this Key Topic you will study:

- collectivisation
- industrialisation
- life in the Soviet Union.

The need for change

Learning objectives

In this chapter you will learn about:
- Stalin's reasons for change in agriculture and industry.

Stalin wanted to make changes in agriculture and industry. He wanted to do this to move the Soviet Union away from NEP policies (that allowed for capitalism) back towards the communism the Bolsheviks had fought for. He also wanted the Soviet Union to be able to compete with capitalist countries, especially those in the West. He wanted the country to become self-sufficient and able to defend itself against any attempt to wipe out communism. This thinking was behind the social and economic changes that he pushed through so fast to modernise the Soviet Union. It would have been easier for the state – and far easier for the people – if the changes had been slower. It is hard to put huge changes into effect without training people for some years to use new systems and new technologies. But Stalin felt the USSR was in danger, so he could not slow down.

Collectivisation and industrialisation

The two major changes that Stalin was relying on to modernise the Soviet Union quickly were collectivisation and industrialisation.

Collectivisation meant uniting all farms into big **kolkhozy** (**collective** farms). The state had encouraged peasants to collectivise since 1917, setting up **sovkozy** (large state farms) to show how collectivisation worked: making the fields bigger and using machinery such as tractors for efficiency. But the revolution had given peasants their own land – they did not want to collectivise. Food shortages meant Stalin needed to control the food supply and to increase production, so from 1928 he enforced collectivisation.

Industrialisation was necessary because industry in the Soviet Union, which wasn't very advanced anyway, had collapsed during the civil war. It soon became clear that Stalin needed foreign 'specialists' to help rebuild industry. Even with their help, it was a struggle. They had to start from scratch in training workers and either had to build new factories or work in old ones that were outdated and dangerous.

People ask if the pace can be slackened. No! To slacken the pace would mean falling behind. And those who fall behind get beaten. Old Russia was continually beaten for her backwardness — her military, cultural, political, industrial, agricultural backwardness. That is why Lenin said on the eve of the October Revolution: 'Either perish, or overtake and outstrip the advanced capitalist countries.'

We are fifty or a hundred years behind the advanced countries. We must make good this distance in ten years. Either we do it, or we shall go under.

Source A: part of a speech made by Stalin to the First All-Union Conference of Industrial Managers, 4 February 1931.

Activities

1 Write a slogan for a banner to get over to the people of the Soviet Union why it is important to modernise. Use the text in the first paragraph to find the reasons. It's a banner – so keep the slogan short.

2 Write a sentence to explain why you think Stalin mentioned Lenin (dead since 1924) in his speech in 1931 (Source A).

58

Collectivisation

Learning objectives

In this chapter you will learn about:
- how collectives were organised
- opposition to collectivisation.

examzone
Top tip

When explaining changes, make sure you use your knowledge to discuss before and after. So if asked how collectivisation changed farming - as in the question opposite, don't just say, *peasants had to meet production targets,* say, *peasants had to meet production targets – before they had grown what they wanted and as much as they wanted.*

Stalin needed the peasants to produce more food – so the workers in the towns had enough to eat, and to export grain to get money to buy machines and materials for industry. Also, he distrusted the rich peasants (*kulaks*) who he thought were enemies of communism. He thought changing farming and village life from small peasant-owned farms working in a traditional way, to large collective farms using modern technology like tractors and combine harvesters would solve all his problems. It would destroy the *kulaks* and increase food production.

Collective farms – *kolkhozy* and *sovkozy*

There were two types of collective farm: *sovkozy* large, state farms run by a manager and *kolkhozy* run by committees of peasants. Both had to farm the way the Commissariat of Agriculture told them. *Sovkozy* often had more facilities, such as nurseries and schools, and were better organised.

All the farms worked in the same way. The land now belonged to the state, and peasants had to meet production targets for their crops. They told the state what their collective needed to feed people and have seed for the next year. The state had to approve this. Peasants could not leave to work in towns. They were organised into 'brigades' of families. On an 80-hectare *kolkhoz*, a brigade was about 15 families. Each person worked a set number of days for the state (usually 140 a year) both on the *kolkhoz* and on jobs like repairing roads. Their hours and the jobs they did were set by the state. The state provided seed and equipment. Tractors and combine harvesters were borrowed from **Machine and Tractor Stations** (MTS). After 1935, peasants got an acre of land to farm for themselves. The state was supposed to provide homes, equipment, food, fuel, clothing, education and healthcare. How much it provided varied – visitors from abroad were always taken to see a good *sovkoz*, well run with excellent facilities.

In the 1920s, there were about 20 million peasant households in Russia, most of them organised into communes. The household was the basic work unit of the peasants as well as the basic social unit. The peasants saw the land as their land, but knew that, to keep it, they had to obey the rules of the commune.

Source A: *from* The Soviet Experiment, *written by R G Suny in 1998.*

The way out lies, above all, in passing from small, backward and scattered peasant farms to united, large collective farms, equipped with machinery, armed with scientific knowledge and capable of producing the maximum amount of marketable grain. The way out lies in the transition from individual peasant farming to collective economy in agriculture.

Source B: *part of Stalin's speech in a 1928 debate on the best way to solve the problems of food shortages.*

Activities

1 You are a Party official preparing a talk about collectivisation. List the ways in which collectivisation will change the peasants' lives.

2 In pairs, read the question and answers below. What level would you mark the answers?

Explain how collectivisation changed how a peasant would feel about the land.

A: *It felt like his land before collectivisation, but not after.*

B: *In his mind it wasn't his land any more. Also, he didn't farm a particular piece of land, he farmed the collective land.*

Source C: *farmers using a new tractor to plough up new land for crops on a collective farm in 1926.*

examzone

Build better answers

Explain how collectivisation changed farming in the 1930s. **(8 marks)**

This question requires an *explanation of change*. It is not enough to describe what collective farming was like in the 1930s; you will need to give examples to show how collective farming was different.

■ **A basic answer (level 1)** will give an example of one or more changes, but without details. (For example: ... *changed to one big farm.*)

● **A good answer (level 2)** will provide detail for the examples. (For example: ...*they changed to one big farm, farmed by several families, not separate farms. They also had to sell surplus crops to the state, not in the market.*)

▲ **A better answer (level 3)** explains at least two changes that collectivisation produced and what made this a change. (For example: ... *they changed to one big farm, farmed by several families, not separate farms and they took the hedges down, which meant they could use tractors and other large machinery. They also had to sell surplus crops to the state, not in the market. This meant the state could now control all the food.*)

▲ **An excellent answer (top of level 3)** would link changes.

Peasant objections

Most peasants objected to collectivisation. As one objector said, 'whoever heard of such a thing, to give up our land and our cows and our tools and our buildings, to work all the time and divide everything?' They disliked being told what to grow and what animals to breed. They did not want to work set hours on set jobs – or to be fined if they did not obey the rules. The peasants who objected most were those with the most to lose – the *kulaks*. They had worked hard under the NEP and made enough profit to take on more land to farm and maybe even to hire workers.

Kulaks were not the only opponents of collectivisation. But state officials did not want to admit that. They wanted to believe the peasants supported the state. So they blamed the *kulaks* for the opposition – after all, they were behaving in a very un-communist way by making profits and hiring workers. But village life was more complicated than that. In some places, *kulak* families were much better off than others, but in many places it was hard to tell the difference.

'We won't even be sure of having enough bread to eat,' someone else said. 'Now, however poor we are, we have our own grain, our own potatoes and our own cucumbers and our own milk. We know we won't starve. But in the kolkhoz, there will be no more potatoes of our own, no more anything of our own. Everything will be rationed out by orders, we will just be like the serfs on the landlord's estates in the old days.'

Source D: *from* Red Bread, *written in 1931 by Maurice Hindus whose family emigrated from Russia to the USA in 1905. Hindus returned to the USSR in 1929 and 1931 to visit the villages near his family's old home and write about life in the Soviet countryside. Here he reports a group of peasants talking about plans to collectivise their land.*

Source E: *collectivisation posters like this were used as anti-kulak propaganda in the early 1930s. The slogan at the top of the first one reads, 'Kulaks Against Grain Collections'. The slogan at top of the second reads: 'The Kulak is the Worst Enemy of Poor Peasants'. The box below it says, 'No Place for Kulaks in Complete Collectivisation Regions'.*

Exam-style question

Explain why many peasants objected to collectivisation. **(8 marks)**

Who were the kulaks?

Some *kulaks* behaved like pre-revolution landlords, thought they were better than the other villagers, and treated their labourers badly. They were hated and feared. But, in many villages, the *kulaks* and the peasants trusted each other. Under the system of village-run **communes** set up after the revolution, land was re-distributed from time to time, depending on the number of people in a household. Households sometimes did well, sometimes not, so how well off they were would vary. Sometimes they might hire help, sometimes not. *Kulaks* were often the most organised or educated and so were respected village leaders.

Resisting collectivisation

When given a choice, many villages did not join a *kolkhoz*. They carried on farming as before, producing just enough to feed themselves. They did not feel responsible for producing enough to feed industrial workers. But the state needed to feed everyone so, in 1928, it began to enforce collectivisation. The peasants reacted badly. Many of them killed their animals and hid their seed, crops and tools. Some burned their homes, rather than let them be taken for collectivisation. Between 1929 and 1933, half the pigs and over a quarter of the cows in the country were slaughtered.

Stalin's reaction

Stalin's reaction was severe.

1   He sent out officials to search for hidden crops, salted-down meat and tools. If they failed (and they did, some were killed trying) he sent in the army.

2   He purged the *kulaks* by 'dekulakisation'. The army went into villages, arrested the *kulaks* and took them to the nearest railway station, to be taken to labour camps. In the years 1930 and 1931, about 600,000 farms were dekulakised. *Kulaks* were sometimes chosen by the village committees, sometimes by the army. Anyone who objected to dekulakisation was automatically counted as one, no matter how poor they were.

3   From 1932 onwards, any peasant who would not join a collective was treated as a *kulak*, even labourers who had no land of their own. People were shot if they resisted arrest. Many did not survive the journey to the camps in the far north of the Soviet Union. Of the survivors, many more died in the first year of life in the camps.

> The peasant struck back. If he was to be forced into a kolkhoz he would go empty-handed and let the government work out how to run it. He sold what was saleable and killed what was killable. In village after village it was the same – the slaughter of animals was appalling. At least half of all the pigs in the country were killed, a quarter of the cattle and even more sheep and goats.

Source F: *from* Red Bread, *written by Maurice Hindus in 1931, following visits to the Soviet countryside.*

Activities

1   You are a state official going to a meeting on collectivisation and preparing for a debate with the peasants.

List the various objections that peasants had to collectivisation.

Compare them to the list you made in answer to Question 1 on page 59. Is there any element of collectivisation on your first list that the peasants do not object to, that you could stress? Underline any that you find.

2   Write a sentence or two to answer each of the following questions.

   a   What was Stalin's main aim in forcing collectivisation through quickly?

   b   What effect does Source F suggest forced collectivisation had?

   c   How would this affect Stalin's main aim?

Did collectivisation work?

> **Learning objectives**
>
> In this chapter you will learn about:
> - the successes and failures of collectivisation.

Was the harsh imposition of collectivisation worth it? It was far from a success, especially in the short term.

Failures

The most obvious failure was the famine of 1932–33. Because the peasants had destroyed their crops and animals, and did not plant enough crops the season before, they were badly hit. About 3 million people starved during the famine. Many people thought Stalin did not help the peasants as much as he could have, to punish them for their resistance to collectivisation.

In many places, the peasants remained resentful of collectivisation. They worked hard enough not to be fined, but no harder. They did not try to learn how to use the new machinery, such as tractors or, after 1931, combine harvesters. They damaged machinery, deliberately or accidentally, through misuse. Peasant resentment and lack of co-operation was so widespread that, in 1935, the state had to introduce a *Kolkhoz* Charter that allowed peasants about an acre of land to grow their own crops on and keep cows and pigs. Collectivisation had not really been accepted as an idea – peasants still wanted their own land.

The new machines were often made too quickly by unskilled workers working to high production targets that did not specify quality. So machinery often had faults and did not work properly from the start. The MT Stations were supposed to fix any problems. However, the workers in some of them were as unskilled as the workers who made the tractors in the first place. This meant there was a lot of wasted machinery.

Successes

By 1935, over 90% of farmland was collectivised. Collectivisation was not a complete failure. On state farms, and some collectives, production improved, people adapted to using machinery and their local MT Stations worked well. More and more young people went to agricultural school and learned how to fertilise the land, grow crops more efficiently and use and maintain farm machinery. By 1935, the steep fall in grain production and numbers of animals began to recover. Of course, this might have happened anyway, if collectivisation had been abandoned and the peasants had gone back to traditional farming.

By 1934, rationing of bread and many other foods ended. Collectivisation made state control of food easier, and that was one of Stalin's main aims in setting it up. The state now kept and distributed the surplus food stocks. Also, the state exported grain to earn foreign currency to buy imports needed for industrialisation. Collectivisation was part of Stalin's plan for industrial growth, with targets set out in the **Five-Year Plans**, because he needed to be able to feed more workers and the country needed the profit from exports.

Year	Grain produced (millions of tons)	Cattle (millions)	Pigs (millions)	Sheep and goats (millions)
1928	63	60.1	22.0	107.0
1929	62	58.2	19.4	107.1
1930	65 (+ or –3%)	50.6	14.2	93.3
1931	56 (+ or –9%)	42.5	11.7	68.1
1932	56 (+ or –10%)	38.3	10.9	47.6
1933	65 (+ or –4%)	33.5	9.9	37.3
1934	68	33.5	11.5	36.5
1935	75	38.9	17.1	40.8

Source A: *agricultural production 1928–35, from state figures (some years the figures were not completely accurate).*

By 1929, the state had enough seed to sow enough food in spring. It had buildings, tools, animals and crops not destroyed worth four hundred million roubles. 36 million hectares of the best farmland was collectivised. Thousands of kolkhozy, vital to productivity, had been formed out of small peasant farms, with their small, fenced areas of land that were hard to use machinery on. By 1930, for the first time in their existence, the Soviets were mainly independent of individual peasants for the vital bread supply.

Source B: *from* Red Bread, *written by Maurice Hindus in 1931 following visits to the Soviet countryside.*

Activities

1 a Turn the information on the successes and failures of collectivisation into two separate lists headed *successes* and *failures*.

   b Underline the points that are to do with the co-operation or non-co-operation of the peasants in one colour.

   c Underline the points to do with state control in another colour.

2 Use Source A to make a graph of grain and animal production 1928–35. Write a long caption for the graph, for a Year 7 class, explaining the way production moved.

Exam-style question

Explain the effects of collectivisation on the people of the Soviet Union.
(8 marks)

Source C: *a propaganda poster from 1932. The big slogan says, 'At the end of the Plan the basis of collectivisation must be completed.'*

Industrialisation

> ### Learning objectives
>
> In this chapter you will learn about:
> - Gosplan and Five-Year Plans
> - the Stakhanovites
> - the achievements of industrialisation.

Stalin wanted to industrialise to make the Soviet Union a strong, self-supporting country (see page 57). Gosplan, the State Planning Committee, set up in 1921, had the job of making industrialisation work. From 1928, it organised Five-Year Plans for industry. This was a 'command' economy, where the state decided what was to be produced, where, and who was to produce it.

The Five-Year Plans

The Five-Year Plans set industrialisation targets. There was a target for the Soviet Union, which was broken down so each factory, or mine, or electricity plant, had its own target. However, targets were constantly reviewed, so that people could feel encouraged when they reached them. This made real planning much more difficult.

To begin with, the Five-Year Plans focused on **heavy industry**, building factories and industrial towns. State propaganda posters for the plans were all over the workers' canteens and factory workshops, as well as charts that showed how well workers were doing.

- *The First Five-Year Plan 1928–32:* set targets for the production of iron, steel, coal, oil and electricity. By the end of 1929, posters were already urging workers to complete the First Five-Year Plan in four years. According to official statistics, it did just that. In fact, the first production targets for this plan were not met until the late 1940s.

- *The Second Five-Year Plan 1933–37:* began early, because of the success of the first plan. It targeted the same industries as the first plan, but also set high targets for tractors and combine harvesters, as well as for extending the railways. With its year's start, and significantly lower targets, it met its targets.

- *The Third Five-Year Plan 1938–41:* was the first to include 'luxury' consumer items such as radios and bikes. It was interrupted by the Second World War breaking out in 1939, and the Soviet Union facing the Nazi invasion in 1941.

For Stalin, socialism meant collectivisation, industrialisation, urbanisation and a welfare system for working people, all without capitalism, carried out and managed by a state controlled by the Communist Party. 'We are advancing along the path of industrialisation,' Stalin told his followers. 'We are becoming a country of metal, cars and tractors.'

Source A: *from* The Soviet Experiment, *written by R G Suny in 1998.*

Source B: *the inside of a factory canteen photographed by the US photographer Margaret Bourke-White. She was taken to see 'model' factories with the best workers. The posters encourage workers to complete the first Five-Year Plan in four years.*

Stakhanov

Alexei Stakhanov became famous during the Second Five-Year Plan. He was a coal miner whose target for a 6-hour shift was 7 tons of coal. In one shift he mined 102 tons (much of the preparation was done beforehand, and other workers loaded and moved his coal). Gosplan publicised his achievement. It encouraged other workers to copy him and not just aim for their production targets, but do even more. Workers who did so got more rations, better housing and other rewards.

Workers set up a Stakhanovite Movement, with groups all over the country that held regular competitions to see who could reach the highest production targets. Stakhanovite workers were sent into factories to encourage production and to explain new production techniques and ways of working, in a move to **mass production** and organising work more efficiently.

Source C: *miners moving trucks of coal in the 1930s.*

Activities

1 In pairs, decide what the main aim of Stakhanovites was. Write a poster slogan to encourage workers to achieve it.

2 Copy the generalisations below, and find two details from the text to support each one (like the activity on page 13).

 a The five-Year Plans got more ambitious.

 b Stalin used propaganda as part of the Five-Year Plans.

3 Think of a reason that might link the two statements below and one other reason why Stakhanovites might be bad for a factory. Write a letter to the factory manager explaining your ideas.

 Statement 1: Stakhanovites were not always popular in factories.

 Statement 2: There was often a rise in absenteeism after a Stakhanovite push in factories.

Build better answers

Describe the key features of industrialisation in the USSR in the 1930s (6 marks)

In this question, you should not only list the key features, but also support your list with factual detail.

■ **A basic answer (level 1)** will give one key feature, but without details. (For example, *...they had Five-Year Plans.*)

● **A good answer (top of level 1)** will provide three or more examples, but still not detailed support. (For example, *... they had Five-Year Plans. The government set the targets. There was lots of propaganda to encourage them.*)

▲ **A better answer (level 2)** will give one developed statement, possibly with undeveloped ones too. (For example, *... they had Five-Year Plans, which were production targets for the whole country. Factories had individual plans they had to follow to make sure country targets were met. Gosplan set the targets and factories had to meet them. There was lots of propaganda to encourage them.*)

▲ **An excellent answer (top of level 2)** will give three developed statements.

66

Achievements

The Soviet state used propaganda to exaggerate the rate of industrialisation and to encourage workers to make even greater efforts. While we have to bear this in mind, it would be wrong to think the Soviet Union had not achieved a remarkable level of industrialisation by 1939. It was strong enough to repel the German invasion in 1941. Unemployment dropped sharply and many people had a higher standard of living. Take one example. In 1929, there were 1,157 people living in temporary huts in Magnitogorsk beginning work on the town. They had no paved roads, no drains, and no electricity. By 1932, there were 100,000 people living there. They had brick-built houses, paved roads, electricity and drains. There were several factories, iron and steel works, shops, a school and a hospital. In 1929, 26 million people were living in towns and cities. By 1939, it was 56 million, almost a third of the population.

Problems

- Workers were aiming for high productivity (which was rewarded, not good quality work).
- The shortages of some materials and goods meant some people took bribes and a black market sprang up, selling goods illegally.
- Many workers were not properly trained. So everything, from the tractors a factory made to the factory itself, were often of poor quality.
- Factories had very few safety features, were seldom designed to be efficient, and had a high accident rate.
- Factory chimneys poured out fumes that often affected the health of the people living nearby.

A good example of these effects is the Stalingrad tractor factory; finished in June 1930. Its initial production target was 500 tractors a month. By the end of September, it had produced 43 in total. The average life of one of these tractors was 70 hours of operation, and then it began to fall apart.

Source D: *propaganda poster celebrating the success of the First Five Year Plan. It shows Soviet production rising sharply, while the economies of capitalist England, France, the USA and Germany decline.*

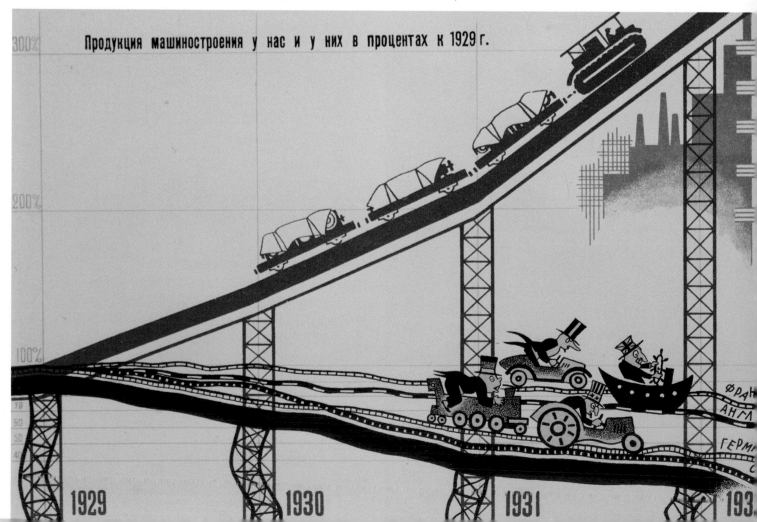

Solving problems

Central control over so huge a country was a problem. Gosplan tried to solve this by setting up a huge **bureaucracy**, but this had its own problems: it was slow and often inefficient. A factory could wait months for the right worker to arrive to mend a machine the person who ran it could have mended, if he had been allowed to.

Gosplan did solve some problems, though. By 1934, Gosplan had seen that quality control was important and had begun to ease off the pressure for rapid production. The Stalingrad tractor factory overcame its early problems. By 1939, it was producing half the tractors in the USSR. Tractor production in the USSR went from 1,300 in 1928 to 50,000 in 1932 to 112,900 in 1936. Many of these tractors worked well over many years.

Industrial production	1928	1936
Iron (millions of tons)	3.3	6.2
Steel (millions of tons)	4.0	5.9
Coal (millions of tons)	35.4	64.3
Oil (millions of tons)	11.7	21.4
Electricity (billions of kilowatts)	5	13.4

Source E: industrial production under the First Five-Year Plan, from state figures.

examzone
Top tip

In your answer to the 16-mark question – like the one on this page – you will be marked on the quality of your writing and on your spelling, punctuation and grammar. There are up to 4 additional marks available for this, so take time to check your writing and ensure it is accurate in spelling, punctuation and grammar.

examzone
Build better answers

Was the lack of skilled workers the main reason for the problems of industrialisation? Explain your answer. (16 marks)

You may use the following in your answer:
- the lack of skilled workers
- the rewards system.

You must also include information of your own.

This question is about *causation*.

■ **A basic answer (level 1)** makes a simple generalisation about causes.

● **A good answer (level 2)** agrees and/or disagrees with the proposition in the question but does not explain how other causes offered were causes. A more complete answer will examine more than two causes.

▲ **A better answer (level 3)** will explain the causes discussed.

▲ **An excellent answer (level 4)** will prioritise the causes, or see links between them (for example, ... *There were a number of causes for the problems of industrialisation and many of them were linked to Stalin's push for greater productivity. So there was a lack of skilled workers and their work was made worse by the emphasis on getting goods out quickly – both the Stakhanovite movement and the government rewards system were focussed on production, not quality of goods. The factories were also a factor – their fumes and their lack of safety features caused a high turnover of workers and the machines were not very efficient either.*).

Activities

1 **a** Draw a graph to show the information in Source E.

b Does it show the Five-Year Plans were a success?

2 Make a table like the one on the right, and fill in the three sections with a series of statements with details to support them.

3 Source D was a propaganda poster used by Stalin's government. Look back over the last 11 pages.

a What impression does this poster give of 1929–32 in the USSR?

b How accurate is this impression?

c Why did Stalin's government use posters like this?

Industrialisation and the 5-Year Plans
Causes
Key Features
Effects

Life in the Soviet Union

Learning objectives

In this chapter you will learn about:
- living and working conditions
- the different experience of social groups.

By 1939, the hardships of the first years of industrialisation and collectivisation were over. A new society was emerging. Was it what the Bolsheviks had hoped for in 1917? The Constitutions of 1918 and 1936 promised social equality, regional equality, freedom of speech and religion, work for all, and hospitals, schools and other facilities for workers. So what was life like in the Soviet Union by 1939?

Social equality

The new society was not equal. There was a huge state **bureaucracy** of officials, all Communist Party members. While Stalin always dressed simply and spoke plainly, he did not live like the workers. He had a flat in Moscow and several homes in the countryside. He ate and drank well and – just like the Tsar – he had a group of officials who were his favourites and who had extra privileges. Most Party workers had a better standard of living than other people.

All groups of workers included people who were in favour with the state and people who were not. Those in favour got rewards – tickets to concerts, days off, extra food, a better job. Those not in favour got worse housing and a much lower place on waiting lists for operations or nursery places. At worst, they became 'enemies of the people' and were sent to camps or to regions such as Kazakhstan.

Ethnic minorities

Stalin's propaganda stressed the equality of the republics of the Soviet Union. Posters and photos show him with people from these regions, often in national dress. Until the early 1930s, the state encouraged local languages in its literacy drives. But during enforced collectivisation the greatest resistance came from the regions, which were heavily purged. From 1932, support for regional identity became seen as 'counter-revolutionary'. The state encouraged 'Russification' – creating a dominant Russian culture. In March 1938, Russian became a compulsory second language in all schools. Russification was patchy and most strictly enforced among groups seen as most likely to resist.

61.3%	lived in a one-room flat
26.9%	lived in a two-room flat
23.5%	had no kitchen
46.5%	shared a kitchen
33.0%	had their own kitchen

Source A: *the statistics above show the living conditions of state officials at the start of 1940. These were not the most important party or government members, but they had better living accommodation than most workers. They were allowed 6.7 sq m per person.*

exam zone
Top tip

When asked *how things changed*, always give factual evidence of what things were like before and after to show the change. So, if asked how Stalin's attitude to the ethnic minorities changed, don't just say, *He stopped encouraging regional differences.* Say, *At first, Stalin encouraged regional differences. He encouraged people to learn to read and write in regional languages, for example. But then he began Russification – making everyone Russian (schools had to teach Russian from 1938).*

Religious equality

In theory, people could follow any religion. In fact, atheism was encouraged; all religion was scorned. People were deported simply for their beliefs, and there were several purges of priests. In 1915, Russia had 54,000 churches. In 1940, there were 500.

Living conditions

New towns may have been built quickly, but the housing, mostly in standard flats, was better than many workers had had before. Even so, most workers had just one room and shared a kitchen with people from other flats. The actual space per person allowed when building flats for workers dropped steadily from 5.4 sq m in 1926 to 4.3 sq m in 1939. This is an average. Officials got more space, ordinary factory workers less.

Activities

1 Draw a graph with the years 1928–38 on the horizontal scale and the vertical scale with *encouraged minorities* at the top and *persecuted minorities* at the bottom. Draw a line to show how Stalin's attitude towards the ethnic minorities in the Soviet Union changed from 1928 to 1938.

2 Use the information in Source A to suggest what the flats in the workers' housing in Source B were like.

Source B: *housing for workers in Chelyabinsk in 1930. The workers were for the tractor factory, already built, just out of the picture.*

Working conditions

Most factories in the early 1920s had a chief engineer (often a foreign 'specialist') and a Red manager (a Party member). From 1928, more and more factories had just one state manager. Some foreign workers were deported, others were allowed in, but they usually worked under a Party manager. The state also stopped free trade unions. Managers could now sack workers and set wages without the factory committee's agreement. Workers usually worked five days then had a day off. The average daily shift was 6–7 hours. The system in mines and steelworks was similar.

In 1934, 'progressive piecework' was introduced. Workers no longer had a set wage, they were paid by the amount they produced. With the rewards system (see page 65) this encouraged production.

Source C: *a poster from 1931. The slogan reads, 'The development of a network of crèches, kindergartens, canteens and laundries, to ensure women can take part in building socialism.'*

Workers, in great demand as industrialisation grew, moved around, looking for better jobs. The state tried to control this by a work passport system where workers could only move with a stamped passport. It hoped this would force workers to stay in one place and learn one job thoroughly. However, work passports were widely forged – in 1937 about 30% of all workers were still changing their jobs every three months.

However, not all jobs were done by workers. Whole canals and infrastructure projects in cities like Magnitogorsk were built using dissidents pressed into service as slave labour.

The role of women

After the revolution, the Bolshevik government introduced several reforms affecting women:

- non-church marriage was set up
- divorce was made simple
- women had equal voting rights to men
- they had equal pay for equal work
- they had equal educational opportunities.

Although women became ever more important in the workforce, the reforms were not enforced. In 1928 there were just under 3 million women working, mostly in farming or as domestic servants. Almost all of those women who worked in factories, worked in textiles (making cloth). By 1940, there were over 13 million women working in all types of industry, including the building industry. They mainly worked at the lower levels, though. Managers were almost always men.

The state needed women to work, especially in factories, because of the huge growth in the number of factories and the desperate need for workers. Women, if they had families, were not likely to move around in the way that men did. The state needed a way to help women work and run their homes. The solution was to provide free childcare until children were old enough to go to school. Free canteens fed the parents at work and the children in nurseries or schools. Free laundries did the washing. There was a problem however: the state did not provide anything like enough, so there were long waiting lists. Childcare was the most important provision – without it women couldn't go to work. As a result many factory nurseries were badly overcrowded.

The Soviet working woman, like all working people, has a seven-hour working day (in many jobs a six-hour day). The principle of equal pay for equal work is strictly observed. The Soviet woman has an annual paid vacation. There are over half a million women working on the railways, many occupy key positions. There are over 100,000 women engineers in industry or in the building trades. In all the other countries of the world combined, there are less than 10,000 women engineers.

Source D: *from* Women in the USSR, *written by M Pichugina in 1939.*

Activities

1 **a** List the ways that the state provided help for women going to work.

   b Often only some of these things were available. Explain how this might make life more difficult for women.

2 Sum up how women's working conditions changed after 1928 in one sentence.

examzone
Build better answers

Explain the effects of the revolution on the lives of women in the USSR.　(8 marks)
This is a question about *consequences*.

■　**A basic answer (level 1)** will make a general statement without any support. (For example: *They got more equality*).

●　**A good answer (level 2)** will make a statement, and support it with some information. (For example: *... there were laws saying they could vote and were equal to men and got equal pay.*)

▲　**An excellent answer (level 3)** will explain at least two effects, with support. (For example: *... the new government passed laws that were all about equality. So women could vote on the same basis as men, and got equal pay for the same work. They got help with going to work, too – there were crèches and nurseries and canteens and laundries. There may not have been enough of these to go round, but this was still a huge change from their lives before the revolution where there was no help provided at all.*)

Source E: *collectives usually had part-time nurseries, open when women were needed at busy times of the year, such as the harvest. These babies have been brought outside as the weather is fine.*

In the Unit 2 exam, you will have to answer six questions: Question 1(a), (b), (c) and (d); either Question 2(a) or Question 2(b); and either Question 3(a) or Question 3(b). You have only 1 hour and 15 minutes to answer these questions.

Here we are going to look at Question 3. You should allow about 25 minutes for this question. In addition to the 16 marks available for this question, there are 4 additional marks available for spelling, punctuation and grammar. Make sure you leave some time at the end to check these aspects of your answer. In addition to the 16 marks available for this question, there are 4 additional marks available for spelling, punctuation and grammar. Make sure you leave some time at the end to check these aspects of your answer.

exam zone

Build better answers

Question 3

Tip: Both Question 3(a) and 3(b) will ask you to use your knowledge to make judgements on causes, effects or importance of factors. In the examination, you can choose to answer whichever of (a) or (b) you like the most. Do not do both (a) and (b) as the examiners will give you marks for only one of them. Remember that this is the highest-scoring question on the paper and requires a substantial and detailed response. You will be spending around 25 minutes on this answer, so you cannot write at enormous length. However, you should:

- use the examples given in the question and at least one of your own
- provide factual information from the sources on the paper and your own knowledge to support what you say about the causes, effects or important features
- make judgements on the relative importance of the causes, effects or important features.

We are going to pick a causation question and work our way through the levels until we have a high level 4 response.

The question we will use is:

Was the Stakhanovite movement the main reason for the rapid expansion of Soviet industry in the 1930s? Explain your answer.

> You may use the following information to help you with your answer.
> - The Stakhanovite movement
> - The role of women

Student answer	Comments
I think the important reasons were the first 5-Year Plan and the Stakhanovite movement.	I am afraid that in a 16-mark question requiring extended writing, this isn't a good answer. The answer mentions two points, one from the examples and one from their own knowledge, so it would be a level 1. It hasn't addressed the question of communication as a main reason, nor has it made a judgement and supported it.

So let's provide that detail. The new parts are in bold.

Student answer	Comments
I think the important reasons were the first 5-Year Plan and the Stakhanovite movement. **The first 5-Year Plan was started in 1928 and it set targets for the basic industries – iron, steel, coal, oil and electricity. Stakhanov was a miner who dug over 100 tons of coal in one shift – he was made a hero and people were encouraged to copy him throughout the USSR, whatever industry they worked in.**	Now we are beginning to get some information into our answer and to write some history instead of the generalised comments made in the previous answer. However, although it provides factual support for the two reasons given, it doesn't suggest how important the reasons were. For example, was one reason more important than the others?

So let's do what the examiner wants. We will put the new parts in bold.

I think the important reasons were the first 5-Year Plan and the Stakhanovite movement, **and the success of the collective farms at increasing food production by the middle of the 1930s, which meant there could be more factory workers.** The first 5-Year Plan was started in 1928 and it set targets for the basic industries – iron, steel, coal, oil and electricity. Stakhanov was a miner who dug over 100 tons of coal in one shift – he was made a hero and people were encouraged to copy him throughout the USSR, whatever industry they worked in. **The most important was the first 5-Year Plan, because it prioritised the key industries and set targets.**	We are getting to a high standard now. The answer has brought in a reason not given in the question (the success of the collective farms), has looked at a variety of factors and decided that one of them (the first 5-Year Plan) was more important than the others. The answer just needs to show the reasons are all interlinked to improve further.

Now let's introduce that linking by adding the following paragraph at the end of the above answer.

The 5-Year Plan set the targets, and without targets Stakhanov could not have been a hero, because he became a hero by beating the targets. Because everyone had targets, everyone could try to beat them. Women could not have gone to work if Gosplan hadn't ordered nurseries to be built to look after their children. Most important, all the other industries could not have grown without the iron and steel and power from the first 5-Year Plan.	Lovely! **Note:** remember that Question 3 is one on which your skills of written communication will be judged and the accuracy of your spelling, punctuation and grammar will be marked. Do your best to write effectively, organise coherently, and spell, punctuate and use grammar with considerable accuracy.

Welcome to exam zone

Zone In!

Have you ever become so absorbed in a task that it suddenly feels entirely natural? This is a feeling familiar to many athletes and performers: it's a feeling of being 'in the zone' that helps you focus and achieve your best.

Here are our top tips for getting in the zone with your revision.

- **Understand the exam process** and what revision you need to do. This will give you confidence but also help you to put things into proportion. Use the Planning Zone to create a revision plan.

- **Build your confidence** by using your revision time, not just to revise the information you need to know, but also to practise the skills you need for the examination. Try answering questions in timed conditions so that you're more prepared for writing answers in the exam.

- **Deal with distractions** by making a list of everything that might interfere with your revision and how you can deal with each issue. For example, revise in a room without a television, but plan breaks in your revision so that you can watch your favourite programmes.

- **Share your plan with friends and family** so that they know not to distract you when you want to revise. This will mean you can have more quality time with them when you aren't revising.

- **Keep healthy** by making sure you eat well and exercise, and by getting enough sleep. If your body is not in the right state, your mind won't be either – and staying up late to cram the night before the exam is likely to leave you too tired to do your best.

Planning Zone

The key to success in exams and revision often lies in the right planning, so that you don't leave anything until the last minute. Use these ideas to create your personal revision plan.

First, fill in the dates of your examinations. Check with your teacher when these are if you're not sure. Add in any regular commitments you have. This will help you get a realistic idea of how much time you have to revise.

Know your strengths and weaknesses and assign more time to topics you find difficult – don't be tempted to leave them until the last minute.

Create a revision 'checklist' using the Know Zone lists and use them to check your knowledge and skills.

Now fill in the timetable with sensible revision slots. Chunk your revision into smaller sections to make it more manageable and less daunting. Make sure you give yourself regular breaks and plan in different activities to provide some variety.

Keep to the timetable! Put your plan up somewhere visible so you can refer back to it and check that you are on track.

Know Zone

In this zone, you'll find some useful suggestions about how to structure your revision, and checklists to help you test your learning for each of the main topics. You might want to skim-read this before you start your revision planning, as it will help you think about how best to revise the content.

Remember that different people learn in different ways – some remember visually and therefore might want to think about using diagrams and other drawings for their revision, whereas others remember better through sound or through writing things out. Try to think about what works best for you by trying out some of the techniques below.

- **Summaries**: writing a summary of the information in a chapter can be a useful way of making sure you've understood it. But don't just copy it all out. Try to reduce each paragraph to a couple of sentences. Then try to reduce the couple of sentences to a few words!

- **Concept maps**: if you're a visual learner, you may find it easier to take in information by representing it visually. Draw concept maps or other diagrams. They are particularly good to show links, for example you could create a concept map which shows the effects of the collectivisation on agricultural production. It would involve arrows pointing to such things as 'land losses', 'military losses' etc.

- **Mnemonics**: this is when you take the first letter of a series of words you want to remember and then make a new sentence.

- **Index cards**: write important events and people on index cards then test yourself on why they were important.

- **Timelines**: create a large, visual timeline and annotate it in colour.

- **Quizzes**: let's face it, learning stuff can be dull. Why not make a quiz out of it? Set a friend 20 questions to answer. Make up multiple-choice questions. You might even make up your own exam questions and see if you friend can answer them!

And then when you are ready:

- practice questions – go back through the sample exam questions in this book to see if you can answer them (without cheating!)

- try writing out some of your answers in timed conditions so that you're used to the amount of time you'll have to answer each type of question in the exam.

If you are sitting your exams from 2014 onwards, you will be sitting all your exams together at the end of your course. Make sure you know in which order you are sitting the exams, and prepare for each accordingly – check with your teacher if you're not sure. They are likely to be about a week apart, so make sure you allow plenty of revision time for each before your first exam.

Know Zone Unit 2B Key Topic 1

You should know about the following things. If you can't remember any of them, just look at the page number and re-read that chapter.

You should know about...

❑ The influence of Rasputin (**page 9**)

❑ What problems Russia had in 1917 (**pages 7–8**)

❑ What groups opposed the Tsar (**page 10**)

❑ How the First World War affected Russia (**pages 11–13**)

❑ Why the February Revolution broke out (**page 14–16**)

❑ How the army reacted to the February Revolution (**page 16**)

Key people and groups

Do you know why these people or groups are important?

Tsar Nicholas II (**page 8**)

the Duma (**page 9**)

soviets (**page 8–10**)

Rasputin (**page 9**)

the Bolsheviks (**page 10**)

Key events

Do you know about the events below? If not, go back to the page and look them up!

Events

The February Revolution
(**pages 12–13**)

The abdication of the Tsar
(**page 16**)

You should know about the following things. If you can't remember any of them, just look at the page number and re-read that chapter.

You should know about...

- ❏ Who was in the Provisional Government (**pages 16–17**)
- ❏ What problems the Provisional Government faced (**page 21**)
- ❏ What stopped the Provisional Government from dealing with its problems effectively (**page 21**)
- ❏ What the Provisional Government did about the war (**page 21**)
- ❏ Why support for the Bolsheviks grew (**pages 22–23**)
- ❏ What effect Kornilov's Revolt had on the Provisional Government (**pages 24–25**)
- ❏ What happened in the October Revolution (**pages 25–27**)
- ❏ Why the Bolsheviks were able to seize power (**page 23**)
- ❏ What the first decrees passed by the Bolsheviks were (**page 29**)
- ❏ What the Bolsheviks did about the war (**page 29**)
- ❏ Which group won a majority in the Constituent Assembly (**page 28**)
- ❏ Who won the civil war and why (**pages 32–33**)
- ❏ What War Communism was (**page 32**)
- ❏ What effects War Communism had (**page 36**)
- ❏ What the NEP was (**page 36**)
- ❏ What effect did the NEP have (**page 37**)

Key events

Do you know about the events below? If not, go back to the page and look them up!

Events

The formation of the Provisional Government (**pages 16–17**)

The July Days (**page 23**)

Kornilov's Revolt (**pages 24–25**)

The October Revolution (**pages 25–27**)

The civil war (**pages 30–31**)

The Kronstadt Mutiny (**page 36**)

Key people and groups

Do you know why these people or groups are important?

the Provisional Government (**pages 16–17**)

the Petrograd Soviet (**pages 16–17**)

Vladimir Ilyich Lenin (**page 22**)

Leon Trotsky (**page 22**)

the Red Guard (**page 23**)

Alexander Kerensky (**page 24**)

General Kornilov (**page 24**)

The Military Revolutionary Committee (**page 25**)

The Council of People's Commissars (**page 26**)

The Whites (**page 30**)

The Cheka (**page 32**)

The Red Army (**pages 30 & 32**)

Know Zone Unit 2B Key Topic 3

You should know about the following things. If you can't remember any of them, just look at the page number and re-read that chapter.

You should know about...

❏ Who the possible successors to Lenin were (**page 41**)

❏ Why Stalin won the leadership (**page 42-43**)

❏ The role of the secret police in the terror (**pages 44–45**)

❏ What the purges were and who was purged (**page 45**)

❏ What show trials were and why they were important (**page 46**)

❏ What the effects of the purges were (**page 47**)

❏ How the state used propaganda (**page 48**)

❏ What the cult of Stalin was (**page 50**)

❏ How the 1936 Constitution was used as propaganda (**page 51**)

❏ How censorship created an official culture (**page 52**)

Key people and groups

Do you know why these people or groups are important?

Josef Stalin (**page 41**)

Lev Kamenev (**page 41**)

Gregori Zinoviev (**page 41**)

The Politburo (**page 41**)

The OGPU (**page 44**)

The Gulag (**page 45**)

Key events and ideas

Do you know about the events below? Do you know what the key phrases mean? If not, go back to the page and look them up!

Events

Trotsky exiled from the USSR, 1929 (**page 43**)

The Great Terror 1936-38 (**page 45**)

Ideas

Socialism in One Country (**page 42**)

'Old Bolsheviks' (**page 46**)

propaganda (**page 48**)

Test your spelling

Remember that in question 3, the accuracy of your spelling is one element of your answer that will be assessed. Make sure you can spell the key events, ideas and people listed above, and the following terms from this key topic:

capitalism	cult
censorship	purge
constitution	socialism

You should know about the following things. If you can't remember any of them, just look at the page number and re-read that chapter.

You should know about...

❏ Why Stalin wanted to modernise quickly (**page 57**)

❏ Why Stalin introduced collectivisation (**page 58**)

❏ Why mechanisation was easier on collective farms (**page 58**)

❏ Why many peasants were opposed to collectivisation (**page 61**)

❏ How Stalin reacted to opposition (**page 61**)

❏ What the successes and failures of collectivisation were (**pages 62–3**)

❏ What the Five-Year Plans were (**page 62**)

❏ What the achievements of the Five-Year Plans were (**page 66**)

❏ Why the emphasis on productivity was a problem (**page 66**)

❏ How Stalin's attitudes to the ethnic minorities changed (**page 68**)

❏ How the role of women changed (**pages 70–71**)

Key events and ideas

Do you know about the events below? Do you know what the key phrases mean? If not, go back to the page and look them up!

Events

Enforced collectivisation from 1928 (**page 61**)

The famine of 1932-33 (**page 62**)

The *Kolkhoz* Charter of 1935 (**page 62**)

Ideas

collectivisation (**page 57**)

dekulakisation (**page 61**)

Five-Year Plans (**page 64**)

Russification (**page 69**)

progressive piecework (**page 70**)

Key people and groups

Do you know why these people or groups are important?

Machine and Tractor Stations (**page 58**)

kulaks (**page 60**)

Gosplan (**page 64**)

Alexei Stakhanov and the Stakhanovite Movement (**page 65**)

Remember that in question 3, the accuracy of your spelling is one element of your answer that will be assessed. Make sure you can spell the key events, ideas and people listed above, and the following terms from this key topic:

agriculture	machinery
atheism	minority
bureaucracy	productivity
commune	self-sufficient
efficiency	sovkozy
industrialisation	Stakhanovite
kolkhozy	Technology

Don't Panic Zone

As the day of the exam gets closer, many students tend to go into panic mode, either working long hours without really giving their brain a chance to absorb information, or giving up and staring blankly at the wall.

Look over your revision notes and go through the checklists to remind yourself of the main areas you need to know about. Don't try to cram in too much new information at the last minute and don't stay up late revising – you'll do better if you get a good night's sleep.

Exam Zone

What to expect in the exam paper

You will have 1 hour and 15 minutes in the examination. There are three questions in the exam paper, and you have to answer all three of them. In Question 1 you don't get a choice – there are four parts to the question (a-d) and you must answer all four. In questions 2 and 3 though, you do get a choice. In each case there are two parts to the question (a and b) and you only answer **one** of them – so either 2a or 2b and either 3a or 3b.

The questions you answer have different numbers of marks available, and we suggest below roughly how long you should spend on each one. The best way to organise your time is to have a few minutes left at the end so you can read through your answers and check your spelling, punctuation and grammar. What you don't want to do, is to run out of time on question 3 – which has the most marks of any question on the paper. One important thing to remember is that the question and answer booklet has lots of lines for each question. This is designed so people with the largest handwriting have room to write a long answer. Don't try to fill all the lines – there are more lines than you will need.

Question 1a is worth 4 marks (about 6 minutes)

It starts with a source written by a historian, and the question asks you what you can learn from the source about something. It could be what you can learn about the impact of an event, or the problems faced, or the reasons for what happened.

Question 1b is worth 6 marks (about 8 minutes)

It asks you to describe something – it could be policies, key features, problems.

Question 1c is worth 8 marks (about 10 minutes)

It asks you to explain the effects of something. Read it carefully, there are two key parts to the question, because, for example, it will ask you to *explain the effects of the February Revolution on Russia in 1917*. Make sure you focus on both key parts.

Question 1d is worth 8 marks (about 10 minutes)

This will be a question about causes. You will be asked to *explain why* something happened. Remember, events in history always have more than one cause, and the causes usually link together. Also make sure you explain why the causes you describe led to the event happening.

Question 2 is worth 8 marks (about 12 minutes)

This is a question about change or development, where you have a choice and answer **either** part a **or** part b. Use the extra couple of minutes to think about both questions and decide which to answer. It might help to jot down the main facts you could use in your answer for each possible question. When you know which one is the best for you to do, remember to use facts to support your answer.

Question 3 is worth 16 marks (about 25 minutes)

This question is usually about causes or effects and it is another one where you answer either part a or part b. It is worth almost one third of the marks for the whole paper. So spend a couple of minutes thinking about which is the best one to answer. It is quite different from the other questions in that it gives you some help in listing things you could use in your answer. This is a good hint. You are also told you must include information of your own. Be sure to use the listed examples and add to them from your own knowledge. Try to give as much detail as possible. Your answer for this question will be marked for spelling, punctuation and grammar: there are up to 4 additional marks available for this aspect of your writing.

Meet the exam paper

In this exam you will write all of your answers in the spaces provided on the exam paper. It's important that you use a black pen and that you indicate clearly which questions you have answered where a choice is provided – instructions will be given on the paper. Try to make your handwriting as legible as possible.

Print your surname here, and your other names afterwards. This is an additional safeguard to ensure that the exam board awards the marks to the right candidate.

Here you fill in the school's exam number.

The Unit 2 exam lasts 1 hour 15 minutes. Plan your time accordingly.

Make sure that you understand exactly which questions from which sections you should attempt.

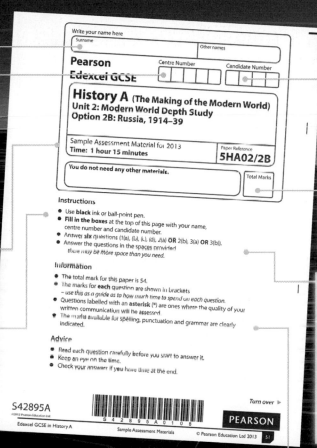

Here you fill in your personal exam number. Take care to write it accurately.

In this box, the examiner will write the total marks you have achieved in the exam paper.

Don't feel that you have to fill the answer space provided. Everybody's handwriting varies, so a long answer from you may take up as much space a short answer from someone else.

Remember that in question 3 your spelling, punctuation and grammar will be assessed, as well as the quality of your written communication. Take time to check your spelling, punctuation and grammar and to make sure that you have expressed yourself clearly.

You need to answer Questions 1, 2 and 3. You should answer all parts of Question 1, but for Question 2 and Question 3, you should answer either (a) or (b).

Russia, 1917–39

Answer Questions 1(a) to (d), then Question 2(a) OR 2(b) and then Question 3(a) OR 3(b).

Question 1 – you must answer all parts of this question.

Study Source A.

Source A: From a history of the Twentieth Century, published in 1999.

> The Russian armies eventually collapsed in 1917, but this was due more to poor leadership, inadequate supplies and political developments at home, than to defeat in the field. Russia's cities experienced food shortages. There was inflation and enthusiasm for the war had been replaced by discontent and waves of strikes. By early 1917 all the ingredients for revolution existed in Russia.

(a) What can you learn from Source A about the problems facing Tsar Nicholas II in 1917?

(4)

Question 1a

When you answer you should always say what the source tells you, and give a reason for it. A good answer to the question above is: *It tells me the Tsar was facing severe problems* [what it tells you]. *It mentions food shortages, inflation and strikes* [the reason].

The number of marks available for each question is given on the right.

Question 1b

A good answer will make more than one point (the question says *features*) and support or explain each point with some detail you can remember, e.g. *one key feature was autocracy* [your point]. *The Tsar believed he alone should rule Russia, and he did not want to share power with a parliament* [your support or explanation].

(b) Describe the key features of the government of Russia under Tsar Nicholas II before the revolution in February 1917.

(6)

(c) Explain the effects of the use of terror by Lenin and Stalin.

(8)

Question 1c

The question says *effects* so make sure you describe at least two effects, and three if you can. Good answers explain how each effect works, e.g. *they both used the Terror to remove political opponents, so after periods of terror they had fewer opponents* [the effect] *and this made people scared and less likely to oppose them* [the explanation].

Question 1d

This is a causation question, so make sure your answer has more than one cause, and for each cause you include explain why it was a cause, or how it worked, e.g. *The Provisional Government decided to continue in the war [the cause] this made the Provisional Government less popular, especially with the troops, and the many deserters. It helped the Bolsheviks seize power because people were willing to support them because they thought the Provisional Government was no use [the explanation].* If you can, show how the causes you write about were linked together.

(d) Explain why the Bolsheviks were able to seize power in October 1917.

(8)

Question 2

Your explanation should always include more than one reason or feature. Make sure you support or explain each feature, and if you can explain how the features link together, e.g. *The big change was from War Communism to the NEP. War Communism had introduced complete government control over food and industry and banks to help win the civil war and destroy all opposition to communism. They thought this was what people wanted, but the Kronstadt Mutiny and the peasants' reactions to War Communism showed them they had changed too much too soon. The state stopped taking grain from the peasants and factories with under 20 workers could be privately owned.*

Answer EITHER Question 2(a) OR 2(b).

EITHER

2 (a) Explain how the economic policies of Lenin's government changed in the years 1918–24.

OR

2 (b) Explain how the role of women changed in the Soviet Union in the years 1928–39.

Indicate which question you are answering by marking a cross in the box ☒. If you change your mind, put a line through the box ☒ and then indicate your new question with a cross ☒.

Chosen Question Number: **Question 2(a)** ☐   **Question 2(b)** ☐

Either 2a or 2b

Remember, this is one of the questions where you have a choice. Look at both parts, and decide which one to answer, then make sure you put an x in the right box to show which question you have answered.

The live question paper will contain one further page of lines.

This asterisk indicates that in this question the quality of your written communication will be assessed. You should always do your best to write neatly and spell and punctuate properly. It's even more important in this question, because some of the marks are for your spelling, punctuation and grammar.

In Question 3 you also have to choose to answer either part (a) or part (b).

Answer EITHER Question 3(a) OR 3(b).

Spelling, punctuation and grammar will be assessed in this question.

EITHER

*3 (a) Was the use of propaganda the main reason Stalin was able to achieve complete control over the Soviet Union by 1939? Explain your answer.

(16)

> You may use the following in your answer.
> • The use of propaganda
> • The purges
>
> You must also include information of your own.

OR

*3 (b) Was the Stakhanovite movement the main reason for the rapid expansion of Soviet industry in the 1930s? Explain your answer.

(16)

> You may use the following in your answer.
> • The Stakhanovite movement
> • The First Five-Year Plan
>
> You must also include information of your own.

(Total for spelling, punctuation and grammar = 4 marks)
(Total for Question 3 = 20 marks)

Indicate which question you are answering by marking a cross in the box ☒. If you change your mind, put a line through the box ☒ and then indicate your new question with a cross ☒.

Chosen Question Number: **Question 3(a)** ☐   **Question 3(b)** ☐

....
....
....
....
....

The live question paper will contain three further pages of lines.

TOTAL FOR PAPER = 54 MARKS

...essment Materials   © Pearson Education Ltd 2013   57

Always remember the marks
Use your time wisely. This question is worth 16 marks, one third of all the marks for this exam.

Make sure you put an x in the correct box to show which question you have answered.

Question 3
This question asks you to make a judgement – *was it the <u>main</u> reason.* You also get some help, in that you get a list of reasons. However, the question also says: *You must also include information of your own.* A good answer must do three things. First, show the examiner you understand a number of reasons. Second, make sure you focus on which was the *main* reason. To do this you need to clearly explain several reasons and explain your judgement. Don't forget to use information of your own in your answer.

Be careful
You should always do your best to write neatly, and spell and punctuate properly. It's even more important in this question, because some of the marks are for your spelling, punctuation and grammar.

Zone Out

This section provides answers to the most common questions students have about what happens after they complete their exams. For more information, visit www.examzone.co.uk.

When will my results be published?

Results for GCSE examinations are issued on the third Thursday in August.

Can I get my results online?

Visit www.resultsplusdirect.co.uk, where you will find detailed student results information including the 'Edexcel Gradeometer' which demonstrates how close you were to the nearest grade boundary.

I haven't done as well as I expected. What can I do now?

First of all, talk to your teacher. After all the teaching that you have had, and the tests and internal examinations you have done, he/she is the person who best knows what grade you are capable of achieving. Take your results slip to your subject teacher, and go through the information on it in detail. If you both think that there is something wrong with the result, the school or college can apply to see your completed examination paper and then, if necessary, ask for a re-mark immediately.

Can I have a re-mark of my examination paper?

Yes, this is possible, but remember only your school or college can apply for a re-mark, not you or your parents/carers. First of all you should consider carefully whether or not to ask your school or college to make a request for a re-mark. It is worth knowing that very few re-marks result in a change to a grade, simply because a re-mark request has shown that the original marking was accurate. Check the closing date for re-marking requests with your Examinations Officer.

Bear in mind that there is no guarantee that your grades will go up if your papers are re-marked. The original mark can be confirmed or lowered, as well as raised, as a result of a re-mark.

Glossary

Term	Definition
abdicate	Give up political power (usually by the ruler of a country).
agricultural production	Crops and animals grown and raised by farmers.
Bolsheviik	The faction of the Russian socialist movement led by Lenin and his supporters.
bourgeois	To do with the middle classes (for example doctors, teachers).
bureaucracy	Groups of officials who carry out government orders and run the country.
capital punishment	Punishing crime by executing the criminal.
capitalist	A person who owns land or factories and makes their money not by working but by selling what workers on the land or in the factories produce.
censorship	Telling the media what they can or cannot print or say.
civil war	War between groups of people in the same country.
collective	Where everyone who works or lives in one place follows a set of rules drawn up by the group.
communes	Groups that run themselves.
communism	A system where everyone is equal, the state owns everything and provides everything that people need.
conscripted	Forced to join the armed services.
counter-revolution	A revolution to overturn a recent revolution (either to replace the system the first revolution overthrew or to replace it with a third system).
coup	Violently overthrowing a government.
decree	Orders that have the force of law.
desert	To leave the army without permission.
heavy industry	Industries such as the coal, oil and iron and steel industries, that produce raw materials for other industries to turn into goods.
industrialised	Having factories and heavy industries (such as iron and steel works) to produce goods and services (such as an electricity supply) on a large scale.
kolkhozy	Collective farms
locked-out	Employers stopped workers from coming into the place where they work.
Machine and Tractor Stations	Places where tractors and other machines are kept and maintained, then lent out to collective farms when they are needed.
martial law	When the normal government is replaced (usually in an emergency) by rule by the army.
mass production	Making goods that have standardised parts (for example, the same sized bolts) to make them quicker and cheaper to produce.

Mensheviik	A faction of the Russian socialist movement who opposed the Bolsheviks and Lenin in the struggle for power after the 1917 Revolution.
mutinied	Refused to obey the orders of those in command, usually in the armed services.

Term	Definition
Five-Year Plans	Plans that set out how much of an agricultural or industrial product should be produced in a year and who should produce it.
political commissar	An official under the Bolshevik government, in charge of making sure important groups (such as the army) stay loyal.
propaganda	Information, true or false, to make people think or behave in a particular way.
sabotage	Deliberately destroying or damaging something in a factory or other workplace.
secret ballot	Voting secretly.
social inequality	Where people are not equal, some are treated differently to others, some are rich, some poor.
soukozy	state farms
Tsar	The title of the ruler of Russia until 1917.

Groups	
Central Executive Committee (CEC)	Elected by the Congress of Soviets as a check on the CPC.
Cheka	The Bolshevik secret police until 1922, who had special powers to arrest and imprison without trial.
Congress of Soviets	The national meeting of representatives from all the soviets.
Constituent Assembly	The government set up by the Provisional Government after the February Revolution of 1917, and elected under Bolshevik Rule after the October Revolution of 1917. It sat only once, before the Bolsheviks replaced it.
Council of People's Commissars (CPC)	The group that ran the early Bolshevik Government.
Gosplan	The State Planning Committee that ran the Five-Year Plans.
Military Revolutionary Committee	The part of the Petrograd Soviet that deal with organising armed support (in the army and elsewhere) for the October Revolution of 1917.
Okhrana	The Tsar's secret police, who had special powers to arrest and imprison without trial.
(O)GPU	The secret police after 1922, who had special powers to arrest and imprison without trial.
Petrograd Soviet	The organisation formed in 1917 which helped the Provisional Government to power in February 1917.
Provisional Government	The government of Russia from the abdication of the Tsar (2 March 1917) to the seizure of power by the Bolsheviks (25 October 1917).
Red Army	The army of the Bolshevik, later Communist, government.
Red Guard	The workers' fighting units set up by the Bolsheviks.

Acknowledgements

Published by Pearson Education Limited, Edinburgh Gate, Harlow, Essex, CM20 2JE.

www.pearsonschoolsandfecolleges.co.uk

Copies of official specifications for all Edexcel qualifications may be found on the Edexcel website: www.edexcel.com

Text © Pearson Education Limited 2013
Typeset by HL Studios, Long Hanborough, Oxford
Illustrated by Peter Bull Studio, AMR Design and David Woodroffe
Cover photo/illustration © **Getty Images**: Time & Life Pictures

The rights of Jane Shuter to be identified as author of this work have been asserted by her in accordance with the Copyright, Designs and Patents Act 1988.

First published 2013

16 15 14
10 9 8 7 6 5 4 3 2

British Library Cataloguing in Publication Data
A catalogue record for this book is available from the British Library

ISBN 978 1 446 90675 0

Printed in Italy by Lego S.p.A

Acknowledgements
The author and publisher would like to thank the following individuals and organisations for permission to reproduce photographs:

(Key: b-bottom; c-centre; l-left; r-right; t-top)
akg-images Ltd: 50; **Alamy Images**: INTERFOTO 9, Interfoto Pressebildagentur 66, Lebrecht Music and Arts Photo Library 41l, The Protected Art Archive 11; **Bridgeman Art Library Ltd**: Klutchis (fl.1932) 63; Corbis: 42, Bettmann 13, 32, 47, 59, Hulton-Deutsch Collection 46, Underwood & Underwood 56, 65, 71; **Getty Images**: AFP 41c, Hulton Archive 6, 41r; **Mary Evans Picture Library**: Alexander Meledin 12, 15; **TopFoto**: 8, 23, 31, 45, 70, Granger Collection 7, 17, 29, 37, 53, 64, RIA Novosti 20, 21, 22, 27, 33, 35, 40, 49, 60, Ullstein 19, Roger Viollet 69

We are grateful to the following for permission to reproduce copyright material:

Tables
Source B page 10 from The Russian Revolution and the Soviet State, 1917-21: Documents (Studies in Russia and East Europe) ISBN-13: 978-0333166093, Palgrave Macmillan; First Edition (Martin McCauley) 1 Jan 1975

Text
Source D page 12/ Source A page 14 from A People's Tragedy: The Russian Revolution, 1891-1924 ISBN-13: 978-0712673273 Orlando Figues, Pimlico 31 Jul 1997. Reprinted by permission of The Random House Group Limited, Copyright © Orlando Figes 1997. Reproduced by permission of the author c/o Rogers, Coleridge & White Ltd., 20 Powis Mews, London W11 1JN, From A People's Tragedy: The Russian Revolution 1891-1924 by Orlando Figes, published by Pimlico. Reprinted by permission of The Random House Group Limited. © 1996 by Orlando Figes. Used by permission of Viking Penguin, a division of Penguin Group (USA) LLC; Source D page 8/ Source D page 33/ Source A page 58/ Source A page 64 from The Soviet Experiment: Russia, The USSR, and the Successor States ISBN-13: 978-0195081053, OUP USA (Ronald Grigor Suny) 26 Feb 1998, By permission of Oxford University Press; Source C page 12 from The Oxford Illustrated History of the First World War ISBN-13: 978-0192893253, Oxford Paperbacks (Hew Strachan) 9 Nov 2000, By permission of Oxford University Press; Source A page 45/ Source A page 52 from Stalin: The Court of the Red Tsar ISBN-13: 978-0753817667 Phoenix (Simon Sebag Montefiore) 16 May 2007; Source B page 49 from Popular Opinion in Stalin's Russia: Terror, Propaganda and Dissent, 1934-1941 Cambridge University Press (Sarah Davies) 2 Oct 1997; Source E page 51 from Joseph Stalin: A Biographical Companion (Biographical Companions) ISBN-13: 978-1576070840, ABC-CLIO Ltd (Helen Rappaport) 13 Dec 1999

In some instances we have been unable to trace the owners of copyright material, and we would appreciate any information that would enable us to do so.

A note from the publisher
In order to ensure that this student book offers high-quality support for the associated Edexcel qualification, it has been through a review process by the awarding organisation to confirm that it fully covers the teaching and learning content of the specification or part of a specification at which it is aimed, and demonstrates an appropriate balance between the development of subject skills, knowledge and understanding, in addition to preparation for assessment.

While the publishers have made every attempt to ensure that advice on the qualification and its assessment is accurate, the official specification and associated assessment guidance materials are the only authoritative source of information and should always be referred to for definitive guidance.

Edexcel examiners have not contributed to any updated sections in this resource relevant to examination papers for which they have responsibility.

No material from an endorsed student book will be used verbatim in any assessment set by Edexcel.

Endorsement of a student book does not mean that the student book is required to achieve this Edexcel qualification, nor does it mean that it is the only suitable material available to support the qualification, and any resource lists produced by the awarding organisation shall include this and other appropriate resources.